THE WEDDING GOWN BOOK

GLOUCESTER MASSACHUSETTS

QUARRY BOOKS

THE WEDDING GOWN BOOK

HOW TO FIND A GOWN
THAT PERFECTLY FITS
YOUR BODY, PERSONALITY,
STYLE, AND BUDGET

ELIZABETH SHIMER

First published in the United States of America by
Quarry Books, an imprint of
Rockport Publishers, Inc.
33 Commercial Street
Gloucester, Massachusetts 01930-5089
Telephone: 978.282.9590
Fax: 978.282.2742
www.rockpub.com

Library of Congress Cataloging-in-Publication Data
Shimer, Elizabeth.
  The wedding gown book : how to find the gown that perfectly fits your body,
  personality, style, and budget / Elizabeth Shimer.
     p.   cm.
  ISBN 1-59253-066-4 (pbk.)
     1. Wedding costume—United States. 2. Weddings—United States—Planning.
I.
  Title.
  GT1752.U6S45 2004
  392.5'4—dc22   2004003630
                                                         CIP

ISBN 1-59253-066-4

10 9 8 7 6 5 4 3 2 1

Design: Mary Ann Guillette
Layout and Production: Mary Ann Guillette
Cover Images: Justina McCaffrey Haute Couture (front cover),
    Ulla-Maija, Inc. (back cover)
Illustrations: Robyn Neild
Text on page 128 from *Blooming Rooms*, Rockport Publishers (2003)
Text on pages 122–123 from *Gem Magic*, Fair Winds Press (2004)
Rockport Publishers would like to give special thanks to Sabrina Murphy
    for contributing dozens of flawless and timeless photos to this book.

Printed in Singapore

To my dad,
who has always
inspired me
to write.

CONTENTS

INTRODUCTION

"Anyone who says it's difficult to find the right man has never had to find the right dress."

—Dorothy Parker

Singer Toni Braxton went the classic route in an ivory duchess satin gown with a crystal bodice and an antique-style diamond tiara. When Cindy Crawford got married for the second time, she chose a Caribbean beach and an easy-fitting minidress that looked both comfortable and sexy. Just a few years later, Kate Hudson, more of a romantic, wore a long-sleeved Vera Wang with a v-neck fur collar. Shortly after that, dramatic Jennifer Lopez chose a frilly, off-white Valentino couture silk and Chantilly lace gown to wear at a California mansion locale.

It's not just celebrities who are using their wedding day to reflect their taste and personality. Rather than simply conforming to the accepted style of the year, brides today have endless options when it comes to wedding gowns. Traditionalists look regal in cathedral trains, while more casual brides wear sleeveless, halter-style dresses or even two-piece, belly-button-baring gowns. And, for those brides who choose out of the way locales as the setting for the ceremony, it's not unusual to see a themed bridal gown, such as one that evokes the Victorian era or the Middle Ages.

Finding the perfect wedding gown is, appropriately, similar to the quest for the best life partner: To find that "perfect fit," you have to shop wisely. You shouldn't fall in love with the first dress you see, but you shouldn't become obsessed with finding perfection, either.

And what a blast you can have trying on all those elegant, gorgeous gowns with your friends around you—it's not uncommon for bridal shops to offer you champagne while you shop—because they want you to feel sexy and special. Your wedding and your bridal gown are simply a celebration of you and your fiancé—and the celebration should begin during the shopping process. One important thing to remember is not to be swayed by the beauty of the first dress you put on. It's easy to fall in love with gown number one, simply because it's so much more elegant and stunning than anything you've ever worn before.

Therefore, good shopping skills are essential when purchasing your dress. *The Wedding Gown Book* will help you answer all the important questions you need to ask before you buy the most expensive dress you'll ever wear. Can you dance in the dress? Will you be happy with the way the gown looks in pictures? Is the dress the most flattering for your body type?

In the end, of course, your wedding gown is not about shopping wisely or even spending intelligently. It's all about how you look and feel on the day of your dreams. Designers, saleswomen, your attendants, your fiancé, your family, and even I, all want your gown to be the one of your dreams. Congratulations and have a blast—both in the stores and on your special day.

Elizabeth Shimer

TOP: *Although not a must, a veil can add elements of beauty and tradition.*
BOTTOM: *Flowers are classic symbols of weddings.*
OPPOSITE FAR LEFT: *Singer Toni Braxton, with her husband Keri Lewis, a musician, is radiant on her wedding day in 2001 in Georgia.*
OPPOSITE LEFT: *A bodice intricately decorated with colorful flowers.*

1 *HISTORY OF THE WEDDING GOWN*

> *"I . . . chose my wife, as she did her wedding gown, not for a fine glossy surface, but such qualities as would wear well."*

—*Oliver Goldsmith*, The Vicar of Wakefield

ABOVE: *Joseph P. Kennedy, the prominent politician, and Rose Fitzgerald, the daughter of the mayor of Boston, on their wedding day in 1914—future patriarch and matriarch of the Kennedy clan.* OPPOSITE: *Jacqueline Lee Bouvier — perhaps better known as "Jackie O."— in full bridal regalia on the day of her wedding to Senator (and of course, future President) John Fitzgerald Kennedy in Newport, Rhode Island, in 1953.*

Today's bride worries about so much—salmon or steak? D.J. or live band? White sheath or princess ball gown? But, until just before 1900, a bride was lucky if she knew even her husband's name before she said "I do." Not only didn't she choose her husband, but she also didn't choose her gown— her parents did (they were also in charge of the matchmaking for the most part). And they didn't spend much time and money picking out her dress just to make her look good. Instead, they were more concerned with either looking prosperous or, *quelle surprise!*, saving the big bucks for the dowry.

So before you start kvetching about how much you're going to spend and how many decisions you have to make, say a little thank you, because we've come a long way, baby. Now we can choose our guys *and* our gowns! But, whether modest or magnificent, simple or sensational, the gown, in this day and age, is supposed to make the bride look her very best.

The history of wedding gowns is also important for today's bride because many of us feel a strong link to our past when we plan our wedding. So let's take a look at how that mission has evolved over the years, from 4,000 years before the birth of Christ in ancient Egypt to a stroll through a Saks Fifth Avenue store today.

WHY "SOMETHING OLD, SOMETHING NEW"?

The rhyme "Something old, something new, something borrowed, something blue, and a silver six-pence in her shoe" originated in Victorian times. Traditionally, the "something old" is a gently used garter given to the bride by a happily married woman. The "something new" can be anything, but it is symbolic of the future. The bride's family is meant to lend her "something borrowed" as a token of their love (she has to return it for good luck!), and "something blue" represents fidelity and commitment. For example, brides in ancient Israel wore blue ribbons in their hair to symbolize their fidelity.

LEFT: *Modern-day wedding gowns are "anything goes." A bride can create her own balance of trend and tradition.*

ABOVE: *Can't decide between a strapless and a long sleeve? Choose both with an asymmetrical style that elegantly evokes Greco-Roman classicism.*
OPPOSITE: *Many modern gowns, like this one that is elaborately decorated with tiny beads, borrow styles from gowns throughout history.*

THE ANCIENT EGYPTIANS

The ancient Egyptians were the first people to regard marriage as a legal relationship. On the day of the wedding there would be a great banquet, where all the guests would eat, sing, and dance. Then the bride and groom would be led to their home and on the way, green wheat would be tossed in the air as a symbol of fertility.

These folks liked their weddings, alright. The affairs were huge, and the bathing, primping, and hours of makeup application enjoyed by the bride were as elaborate as the light and flowing pleated linen gown she was likely to wear.

THE GREEKS AND ROMANS

In ancient Greece, fathers and uncles arranged a woman's marriage and often offered a dowry to the husband. A girl could be spoken for after the age of five and then married at 15, often to an older distant relative. A torchlight procession took the bride from her house to the house of her husband, where the marriage was consummated. Outside the bedroom door, singing and dancing accompanied the consummation. Weddings for these people were yet another opportunity to pay homage to their numerous gods, as virtually every aspect of the wedding ceremony tipped a hat to the heavens in some way. Even hairstyles were godly; the most popular hairstyle for a bride featured six braids to mimic the 'dos worn by the vestal virgins. And then there was the headpiece—a wreath consisting of lilies, wheat, and rosemary to symbolize purity, the bride's fertility, and the groom's fertility, respectively. At the back of the bride's dress, more- over, which usually was a tuniclike garment white in color to symbolize joy, was a Herculean knot that the groom would untie as the ceremony unfolded.

In ancient Rome, a bride wore her dress only once, just as today's brides do (but not those of the Middle Ages and the Victorian era). Her *flammeum*, or flame-colored veil, was probably the most symbolic thing she wore. In fact, the word nuptial is related to the word nubo, which meant "I veil myself." The veil was oblong and transparent and matched her shoes. The veil left her face uncovered. She also wore a wreath of fragrant flowers. Her gown consisted of a *tunica rectum*, a white flannel or muslin tunic made on an old-fashioned upright loom, and a *cingulum*, or girdle.

There was a knot at the waist of her dress tied to avert ill fortune.

By the way, here's an idea: Roman ceremonies could take place even if the groom was not present. He could actually just write a letter instead, stating his intention.

THE MIDDLE AGES

Despite the economic and political darkness of these times, marriage ceremonies were actually quite cheery, with wedding parties frequently wearing
bright colors such as red, gold, and silver—a practice reflected in the pref-
erence many brides continue to show today for vibrant and well-coordinated
colors. This period also saw the first all-white wedding gown, worn by
Princess Philippa, the daughter of Henry IV of England, who married
Eric of Denmark in 1406. And although the idea of marrying for love was
still a few centuries off, the sentiment at least began to appear in the poetry
of those times—better than nothing, Philippa no doubt thought.

Nobility wore grand and brightly colored robes and gowns often made
of silk. Seamstresses used gold and silver thread to embroider elaborate
designs from legend, nature, or religion. Often the garments were studded
with gems. Then, to top off the clothing, the wedding party and wedding
guests would cover themselves in jewelry, furs, and elaborate belts. Wigs
made from the hair of peasants became very popular.

At that point, of course, all gowns were handmade and designed specifically
to reflect a lady's stature—or to play down physical defects. Gowns made
for Queen Anne Boleyn, Henry VIII's infamous second wife, always
included long sleeves to hide the sixth finger she had on each hand.

THE EIGHTEENTH AND EARLY NINETEENTH CENTURIES

During the French Revolution the textile industry in France suffered.
Emperor Napoleon stopped the import of English textiles and revived
the Valenciennes lace industry so that fine fabrics such as tulle and
batiste could be made in France. To make women buy more material,
he forbade them to wear the same dress more than once to court.
Dresses had extra fabric gathered at the back, and trains were seen again
for evening. Bonaparte also had fireplaces at the Tuileries blocked up
so that ladies would wear more clothing to fend off the cold. He did not
ignore men's role in the revival of the textile economy—he forced male
military officials to wear white satin breeches on formal occasions.

Brides typically wore narrow, high-waisted garments known as "Empire"
dresses (in honor of Napoleon's fated aspirations), accompanied by a
small lace veil on the back of their heads. The Empire dress, which
emerged in the late 1700s, began as a chemise shift gathered under the

breasts and at the neck. By 1800, it had a low, square, décolleté neckline, a short narrow-backed bodice, and a separate skirt. The small, neat, puff sleeves barely capped the shoulder. They were pulled back by the narrow cut of the bodice, which restricted arm movement to a certain daintiness. And much to many grooms' delight, petticoats and corsets fell by the wayside during these times, eliminating some complications of the night for impatient hubbies.

Regency dress during the period from 1800 to 1820, very common in the United States, was based on classical principles of flowing Grecian robes. Until 1810, a tucker or simple *chemisette* (a half blouse that opened on the side) modestly covered the bare neckline by day. These soft muslin dresses clung to the body, highlighting the body's natural outline, so stays were unpopular unless the bride's figure demanded them.

THE INDUSTRIAL REVOLUTION

With the industrial boom came greater personal wealth for many, which was enjoyed primarily by men. Although women began celebrating their femininity, it came at the expense of independence. Women moved in the direction of becoming decorative objects, and their wedding gowns reflected this—with hoopskirts so massive they had to be lowered from the ceiling to be donned. Thankfully the advent of railroad travel made these tents a bit of a squeeze, and they were soon replaced by a narrower and more practical style with a bustle in the back. Nonetheless, a heightened interest in

BELOW: *A corset bodice can help define the waistline... and add old-world charm.*

ABOVE: *This Victorian-inspired wedding gown of ivory satin taffeta is a one-of-a-kind creation, designed in 1993.*

fashion remained. Women began browsing catalogs for not just one wedding dress, but two—the other for social occasions once the ceremony was over. During World War I, Congress gave its approval to exempt wedding gowns from government clothing rationing, so brides still had the latitude to adorn themselves to their heart's desire.

THE 1920s

The trend toward greater practicality, started during the Industrial Revolution, continued into the 1920s, with skirt and dress lengths in general roaring up to just below the knee, a style soon picked up by Chanel in its wedding gowns. For the most part, these shorter gowns maintained a certain elegance by being pure white. A rule of thumb soon emerged, however, whereby the shorter the gown, the longer the veil, thus making way for extraordinary laces and trains. Wedding fashion also began keeping an eye on Hollywood, with many styles reflecting what actresses in the most popular films wore.

THE 1930s

Wedding gowns nearly got put on mothballs with the financial hardships during the Great Depression, forcing many women to wear their best party dress for their big day. These hard times began to lift by the middle of the decade, however, and styles emerged to reflect what was being worn by the rich and famous in Europe. Women began shopping for headpieces in styles similar to the tiara worn by Princess Marina at her wedding to the Duke of Kent (a union that was as celebrated in 1934 as that of Princess Diana to Prince Charles in 1981), and wedding dresses for the first time became available from such department store giants as Lord and Taylor, John Wanamaker, and Bonwit Teller.

WORLD WAR II

A serious wrinkle in the wedding dress industry occurred during the Second World War, and not just because fabric options were limited by the need for silk in the manufacture of military parachutes. Many wives-to-be felt it their patriotic duty either to postpone their weddings or to reduce them in scale, meaning something already in the closet would have to do. Many brides even wore suits, or they rented or borrowed more traditional garb. And, because so many grooms wore uniforms, the focus of the wedding was much more communal and patriotic.

THE 1950s

With the world safe again, the extravagant wedding was reborn, given even more impetus by a blossoming economy and lots of all-too-eligible bachelors looking to settle down. Grace Kelly's much-celebrated wedding to the Prince of Monaco added to the marital fervor and also elevated matrimonial fashion, as women strove to emulate Kelly's peau de soie and lace masterpiece.

The glory of weddings was celebrated not only in the press but also in the movies, especially in such films as *Father of the Bride*, starring Spencer Tracy and Elizabeth Taylor.

THE 1960s AND '70s

The opulence of the '50s ruled until the mid-1960s. With resistance to the Vietnam War came a counterculture more interested in cotton peasant dresses and paisley headbands than in frills and lace. Many couples even moved from the churches and cathedrals to the wheat fields and beaches to tie their marital knots. Brides wore daisies in their hair, and some painted flowers on their faces. It became fashionable to go barefoot and shun makeup during the late '60s. Hillary Rodham wore an off-the-rack Gunne Sax dress designed by Jessica McClintock when she married Bill Clinton on October 11, 1975, in Fayetteville, Arkansas.

By the early '70s, the mod scene brought vibrant colors to the wedding party, and it wasn't uncommon to see ladies in lime green, bright pink, and lemon yellow heading up the aisle.

THE 1980s

Fitting it would be that this era of excess would coincide with the much-ballyhooed merger of Princess Diana and Prince Charles, who married on July 19, 1981. Despite being just 19, Diana was adorned in the most mature of riches, including antique lace, bows, sequins, and thousands of pearls—a style that influenced weddings even in middle America for at least the next 10 years.

This decade saw a return to the huge dress—puffy sleeves and shoulders, balloon skirts, and lush fabrics. At this point in time, the idea of borrowing a dress or wearing an antique dress would have been horrifying to most brides, as the '80s began an era of weddings with budgets that matched the size of the dresses.

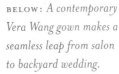
BELOW: *A contemporary Vera Wang gown makes a seamless leap from salon to backyard wedding.*

the wedding gown book

THE 1990s

By the early '90s, extravagance had begun to give way to personal expression and personal responsibility, as many couples started relieving their parents of the financial burden of their unions. Dresses began to reflect a concern with body-consciousness rather than financial opulence. Thus, when Carolyn Bessette wed John F. Kennedy Jr., her slinky sheath was cut to fit her body like a glove (albeit a finely lined one). Likewise, as wedding gowns became less ostentatious and hence less costly, they also started to break new ground in self-expression. Shades such as cream, pink, and even blue began breaking the old color barrier of plain white.

BRIDES TODAY

So where has all this history brought us today? To a place where anything goes. Brides today base much of their decision-making about what to wear not on what is in style but, rather, on what looks good on them. Brides are older now (average age: 26) than ever, and more and more of them trust their own sense of style rather than that of the world of fashion. Dresses can be as simple as a Vera Wang silk or as elaborate as a Priscilla of Boston lace confection and still look both timely and timeless. Pale colors such as pink and blue, or white gowns with deep-colored ribbons, look right at home in a church or at a reception.

And it's not only her sense of style that dictates what a bride will wear. More and more couples are choosing destination weddings and flying their guests to Hawaii, Barbados, or other far-flung locations, rather than marrying in their hometown. In that case, gowns are chosen to suit the setting.

The choice of styles, fabrics, and colors brides have today is wider than it has ever been. So whether you want to be traditional or radical, formal or funky, the green light is yours. Your only duty should be to wear the dress of your dreams.

RIGHT: *Actor and comedian Adam Sandler poses with his bride, model and actress Jackie Titone, at their Malibu, California, wedding in 2003.*

Glimpses of the Past

ABOVE: *Ivory silk peau de soie with lace bodice.*
1955–1957.

the wedding gown book

ABOVE: *Ivory satin with bead embroidered bodice*
and lace collar. Early 1940s.

ABOVE: *Poly-chiffon empire waist with lace appliqué. 1969–1972.*

ABOVE: *Henri Edouard Neveux and Marie Anne Brunelle, June 16, 1920*

ABOVE: *John Ahern and Theresa Buckley, March 17, 1916*

Vintage family portraits

FAR LEFT: *Gerald wore his navy uniform when he wed Barbara just a month after D–Day, creating a picture perfect display of pride and commitment.*
LEFT: *Nearly 60 years later, their granddaughter Kate and Christopher celebrated on the grounds of the Merian Cricket Club near Philadelphia, a location that evoked more of the family's personal history than a specific historical moment.*

RIGHT: *You don't have to be wearing your mother's gown to feel a connection to your family's past. However, this 1969 bride did just that: She donned the dress her mother wore, 30 years earlier, for her own wedding.*

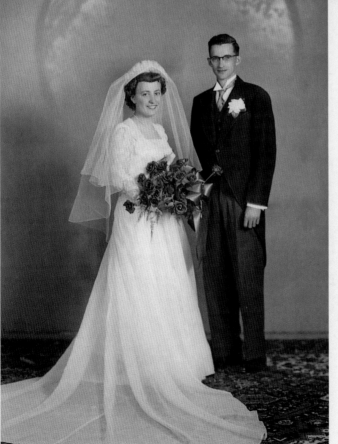

Wedding portraits of three generations of a French-Canadian family:

TOP LEFT: *This late-Victorian era couple, Joseph and Malvina, wore wedding clothes that most likely doubled as their Sunday best.*

TOP RIGHT: *Their daughter, Aline, opted for a gown that reflected contemporary fashions for her 1927 wedding to Eugene.*

FAR LEFT: *Eugene and Aline's eldest daughter Rachel's full length, full coverage, satin and chiffon gown embraced the post-World War II style—proper and elegant—for her marriage to Robert.*

"I wanted the Duchess of York's sense of fun and joy to come out in the dress. One day I woke up in the middle of the night and had dreamed it, and that was it."

—Linda Cierach, designer

You've just said yes to the man of your dreams, and your head is spinning. You're ecstatic, you're in love, and you're about to be married. Life is good. Now comes the really fun part—finding the gown.

It can be tough to focus at a time like this, but you must! And you must also do your homework. Life in the boutiques and bridal salons will be a whole lot easier if you know a sweetheart neckline from a halter.

Here's a crash course to help you map out the road to the perfect wedding gown before you traverse it. We'll discuss silhouettes, bodices, trains, sleeves—if it has ever been associated with a wedding gown, we'll talk about it. Here we go!

SILHOUETTES

Your gown silhouette will be your outline, the shape you will take on the most special day of your life, so this isn't a decision to make lightly. While your silhouette will most likely follow your own shape (see Chapter 4: Flattering Your Shape), rest assured that all body types have many silhouettes from which to choose.

ABOVE: *Here's a sleek and fresh take on the empire waistline.*
OPPOSITE: *Attention to the details, such as these well-designed, satin-covered buttons and the single satin rose on the skirt, create uniqueness, beauty, and style.*

A-line

It's no surprise that A-line gowns are the most popular—they're the most forgiving. Whether you're tall, short, curvy, or straight, an A-line gown, which gently flares from the shoulders on down, will make you look fabulous. A-line gowns can be made in any material and offer a wide variety of bodice styles. Although the silhouette isn't dramatic, the choice of embellishments can add lots of style and personalization.

Ball gown

Think Cinderella. Ball gowns accentuate the feminine hourglass shape, with a narrowly fitted waistline and a full, flowing skirt. Waistlines on a ball gown may be v-shaped, natural, slightly higher than natural, or lower on the hips. Ball gowns often look best on tall women who can carry off the round shape of the skirt. On short women, the skirt often doesn't have enough length to look elegant.

Empire waist

Empire waists are cut sort of like a maternity dress, with a high waistline that starts just below the bust. The skirt is usually slender and graceful. Despite a likeness to a "mother-to-be," empire-waist gowns are some of the most elegant, figure-flattering styles available. It is especially flattering on smaller-busted women, because it gives the breasts some lift and brings the viewer's eye toward the neckline.

Mermaid

Picture just that—a mermaid. This style is slim, sexy, and body hugging down to the knees or just below the knees, where the skirt flares out. This is an unforgiving style—in terms of fitness, that is—and is best reserved for women who are either gently curvy or who love their full-figured voluptuousness.

Princess

On a princess-style dress, vertical panels of fabric follow the natural contour of the body. This is slightly more dramatic than an A-line design, but it is just as easy to pull off, and can be personalized with fabric and adornments, such as embroidery, beading, or lace.

Sheath

Simple and elegant, sheath dresses follow natural body curves from shoulder to hem. They often cling to the body, and many are strapless or even backless. When considering a sheath, you should consider your body an athletic and noncurvy one, as hourglass figures will change the shape of these dresses. Sheaths look fabulous on women of all heights, but the sheath-adorned bride definitely needs to be buff and lean!

LEFT: *This mermaid silhouette accentuates graceful curves, and the baby blue gloves add the perfect touch of color.*
BELOW: *This gown has simple princess lines, but the pleating and high sheen give it an air of drama.*

LENGTHS

Whether you want to glide down the aisle with a mile-long train like Princess Diana or show some leg in a mini, there are plenty of gown lengths available for you to choose from. Etiquette dictates that the time of day and the year of the wedding helps decide the gown length, but don't let those rules stop you from making a certain choice. Instead, just take the rules into consideration when making your decision.

LEFT: *This classic, strapless, floor-length gown is fitting for an afternoon or evening wedding.*
BELOW: *This street-length bridesmaid gown is perfect for a daytime wedding, especially with an outdoor reception.*

Asymmetrical	For the bride who's having trouble deciding on a length, an asymmetrical dress features one side longer than the other. This is a dramatic look and is best for a sophisticated, nighttime wedding.
Ballerina length 	Ballerina-length skirts fall just above the ankle and are usually wider and fuller. They are suitable for all times of day and night.
Floor length	Floor lengths don't fall all the way to the floor, but ½" to 1" (1 cm to 3 cm) from it. These are more formal styles and work best for evening weddings, although they are common in the afternoon, too.
Intermission length	Intermission-length skirts are shorter in the front than in the back, but not by much (we aren't talking a minidress with a bustle and train down the back). This is a simple style and works well in the afternoon.
Mini	For the more daring bride, there is short, short, short! Women often choose this length for daytime, informal weddings or as a second dress to wear at the recep-tion. (It has become fairly common for women to wear a more formal gown during the ceremony and a sexier outfit for the party afterward.)
Street length 	For the practical bride who doesn't want to have to lift up a skirt every time she takes a step, street length skirts fall just below the knee. Although this can be a flattering length for most women, it rarely looks like a wedding gown, simply because it is a length that is so often seen in business suits and casual dresses. Brides marrying for the second or third time may choose to wear street-length dresses.
Tea length 	Slightly longer than street length, tea-length skirts are hemmed at the lower calf or mid-ankle. This is a great length for smaller women, because it doesn't overwhelm the figure with too much material. It also works well for late-morning or afternoon weddings, where it has a more informal look than a longer gown.

ABOVE: *Asymmetrical lines add drama, yet wrap the body tightly, in this modern taken on a Grecian-style column dress.*

SKIRTS

Even though most dresses are one piece, they are divided into two sections: the bodice (the top, including the neckline, sleeves, and waistline) and the skirt. This is one reason why it's so important to understand the language of clothes design, because if you like the skirt of one dress and the bodice of another it is often possible to combine the two looks into a brand-new dress. However, you must have an awareness of how one section will look when combined with another.

From sleek to hoop style, the skirt on your dress will contribute largely to your overall look.

Bouffant		This *Gone with the Wind* style has a very full skirt (if you're daring, possibly even with a hoop). It is best worn on women with long legs. Although you may think that wide-hipped women can use this style to hide extra weight, in fact, the shape only works if it isn't completely filled out by a body underneath.
Box pleated		Deep, parallel pleats of fabric cascade down the skirt. This style can be very forgiving and dramatic, especially when it's done in a heavy satin. Simple, unadorned satin or other smooth fabrics can be made to look lush with this cut and design.
Bustled gown		Fabric is gathered below the waistline in the back of the dress to create fullness. Lifting the train to the waistline and attaching it to the back of the dress with buttons or hooks is another popular way to create a bustle. While many women shy away from bustles, thinking they will draw attention to their butts, the style is actually very flattering for women of all shapes and sizes. The design also allows a woman to have a train for the ceremony and then raise it for the reception so she can dance and move more comfortably.
Pickup hemline		Graceful and elegant, this skirt features pieces of fabric that gather and drape in a curve to one point, then another point, several times all around the dress. This line brings the eye down, away from the center of the body, which can make a small woman look taller and a heavy woman look leaner.
Riding coat skirt		This style features two skirts in one: An overskirt covers an A-line skirt from the back to just past the hips, where it opens to reveal a skirt underneath. This can be done in a demure manner to reveal two wonderful fabrics, or it can be done as a sexy look with see-through chiffon or lace as the underskirt.
Trumpet skirt		Sophisticated and flirtatious at the same time, the skirt is slim and hugging until it reaches mid-thigh, where it flares out. It isn't always easy to move in, because the upper part of the skirt is tight. This style is best for very formal weddings.

ABOVE: *An airy, tulle, bouffant skirt can make a bride feel weightless.*
LEFT: *Creative and elegant, this box pleated skirt cascades beautifully to the floor.*
OPPOSITE: *A bustled skirt creates a dramatic backline and allows the bride to have a formal train during the ceremony and a more comfortable raised skirt for the reception.*

NECKLINES

The neckline of your dress will frame your smiling face and allow you to show as much or as little of your upper body as you wish. When considering your neckline, take into account how much you'll want to move around during your special day (lace and chiffon sleeves can make motion awkward), how much you sweat (sorry to be blunt, but, let's face it, you want to be comfortable!), and where the actual ceremony will take place. Many religious establishments prefer you to save the sexy plunge for the party afterward.

ABOVE: *The bertha-styled neckline on this black bridesmaid's dress adds sophistication to the bodice. This dress would look wonderful at a black-tie Saturday night affair.*
RIGHT: *This sweetheart strapless neckline is romantic, and the black choker adds an element of drama.*

the wedding gown book

BELOW:

TOP: *A contessa neckline flatters a long, slender neck and a defined collarbone.*
MIDDLE: *Sleek, sexy, and informal, halter necklines are comfortable, and they tastefully display shapely arms.*
BOTTOM: *This lace illusion high neckline is sexy and formal at the same time.*

Bateau *(also called a boat neck)* 	A bateau neckline comes to just below the collarbone and goes straight across the chest, following the natural curve of the collarbone. This can be used with or without sleeves and looks best on women with larger busts (but not broad shoulders).
Bertha 	Bertha necklines are close to being off the shoulder, but not quite. The bertha has a wide collar that crosses in front of the bust. This looks best on smaller-busted women, because it creates the illusion of depth and cleavage.
Contessa 	An off-the-shoulder neckline, the contessa attaches to the sleeves to form a continuous line across the arms and chest when the arms are down at one's sides. This is an elegant look that flatters long, slender necks and well-defined collarbones.
Halter 	Made just like the top of the same name, a halter neckline has two pieces of fabric that go up from the waist or bust and join at the back of the neck. This is a sleek, sexy, informal look, although more women are opting for this neckline because they work so hard to create buff arms! This neckline can be seen in lace and in satin, and it works well only if you don't need a bra. (There are halter-style bras, but it's a look that works best on smaller-busted women.)
Illusion high 	This neckline, made of sheer fabric, fits snugly against the neck with an ornately decorated band of satin, creating a choker effect. Quite a formal look, this neckline gives the illusion of sexiness without being over the top.

Jewel

Jewel necklines are high cut and circle the base of the neck. This, too, is a very formal look and works best for a nighttime wedding.

Off the shoulder

With an off-the-shoulder neckline, the sleeves sit at the upper part of the arm, so the shoulders are exposed. This allows the dress to be a bit sexy but usually includes sleeves, so less skin is exposed than with a sleeveless gown.

Portrait

On a portrait neckline, a shawl-like collar wraps around the shoulders. These bodices are often chosen because they frame the face beautifully, making a bride look gorgeous.

Scoop

Scoop necklines are softly rounded and slope downward across the collarbones or bustline. This is a more demure look (when done properly) than a strapless bodice, as long as it's not cut too deeply. A scoop neckline is flattering to almost all women's shapes.

Sleeveless

Surprise, surprise: no sleeves. Instead, the back and front of the gown attach at the shoulder with narrow pieces of fabric. You can only pull off a sleeveless gown if your arms are in perfect shape. This style is quite popular these days, because the look is sexy and carefree, yet sophisticated and fresh.

Square

A square neckline is similar to the scoop, but more elegant and formal. Square necklines work well for almost anyone.

LEFT: *The scoop neckline on this classically beautiful gown creates a more demure look than a strapless bodice does.* OPPOSITE: *A satin portrait neckline on a fuller bust creates a sensual, dramatic look.*

Strapless

In a strapless dress, your arms and shoulders are completely bare, and you rely on gravity and a darn good strapless bra to keep yourself covered. Strapless dresses may or may not have what's known as a crumb catcher, an extra panel of fabric that attaches to the top of the bodice and sticks out slightly from the body. Strapless dresses are all the rage these days.

Sweetheart

One of the most popular shapes, the sweetheart neckline dips down to a point into the cleavage. This is a romantic style that allows for a daring plunge but more demure shoulder coverage. It is flattering to all women and bust sizes.

U-scalloped

U-scalloped necklines are just that—U-shaped and embellished with scalloped lace or appliqués. These necklines rely on design to bring drama and a sense of style to the dress.

V-neck

V-shaped necklines create a V that plunges subtly or sexily into the cleavage. These necklines are very flattering to larger-busted women, because they create an optical illusion that minimizes breast size.

ONE WOMAN'S STORY

When I found out I was pregnant, my wedding was only a month away, and I began to worry about fitting into my dress. But since it had an empire waist, and I still had two fittings to go, I was optimistic that it would accommodate my growing body. After all, at that point, I had barely gained a pound. As the date grew closer, my weight didn't change much, but my bosom seemed to grow larger by the day. Ten days before the wedding, the dress fit perfectly. Four days before, I was pouring out of the dress, and not only did it feel awkward, but it looked ridiculous—not at all what I had envisioned for my wedding day. Unfortunately there wasn't any additional material to let out, so I had no choice but to find another dress. I started to panic as I glanced around at the hideous gowns in the bridal salon—there was no way I would even consider wearing any of them. I adored the dress I had chosen—the tasteful, embroidered leaves flowing down the back of the gown, the soft shade of ivory, the simple lines. Not to mention the equally disturbing thought of spending more money on a second gown!

But I truly was blessed that day. The seamstress disappeared into the back room, and returned a short time later with a sample of my gown left over from the previous year. It was a size 12—far bigger than even my pregnant body required, but we could work with it. Over the next two days, she worked late into the night, placing bones in the front, and taking in what seemed to be yards of material, even though her husband was sick and in the hospital at the time. The night before the wedding, I came to her shop, and she made even more last-minute adjustments. Not only did she go to so much trouble, but she didn't even charge us for the new dress. I was incredibly fortunate to have found such a kind, generous woman, and I looked even better than I had hoped for when my newly voluptuous body made its way down the aisle.

–Davin O'Brien, New York

BACKLINES

Although you may not think about it, from your walk down the aisle to your first dance, your guests will see a lot of the back of your dress, so it should look stunning. At the same time, backlines can create a real sense of personal fashion, from a romantic (yet sexy) corset-style lace-up to a plunging, skin-tight sheath. While you're considering what backline you might like, think too about the type of veil you want to wear. A long, exotic veil will cover up an extreme, backless dress, while a too-short veil might make the look awkward, detracting from both pieces. There is, of course, a world of backlines from which to choose.

LEFT: *Backlines create a sense of personal style. This backless, empire waist gown will leave a lasting impression as the bride walks down the aisle.*
BELOW: *The attention to detail on this satin buttoned scoop backline is polished and refined.*

Backless

For the bride who dares to bare, a backless dress will provide very little coverage and support in the back. Backless backlines are common on halter dresses, as well as other contemporary styles.

When considering whether to wear a backless dress, you should take into account the health (as in "look") of your back. Clear, blemish-free skin and good muscle tone are a minimum. Still, nothing makes a more dramatic entrance into a wedding than a backless dress (because, as I said above, people will be looking at your back as you walk down the aisle and throughout the ceremony).

Keyhole

With a keyhole backline, a peekaboo-style cutout in the back of the gown exposes a section of skin without baring the whole shebang. This look is quite flirtatious without being too risqué.

Scoop

A scoop backline is similar to a scoop neckline, except fabric drapes gracefully across the back in a curve. A modest and pretty look, the scoop backline flatters short hairstyles and women who don't want to wear a long veil.

Surplice

With this style, two panels of fabric overlap at the waist and come up to the shoulders in a V shape. An elegant look, this backline can be created with satin, as well as with gatherings of chiffon for a more Grecian look.

RIGHT: *A gown that's simple and understated in the front can afford to display a plunging V-neck, sequins, and buttons in the back.*

SLEEVES

Different women have definite sleeve preferences. Some women feel free in sleeveless dresses; some feel naked. Some women wouldn't be caught dead in a capped sleeve (it makes their upper arms bulge), while others only feel secure with sleeves coming as close to their wrists as possible. And, as mentioned in Chapter 1, Anne Boleyn insisted that her sleeves come down past her fingers to hide the fact that she had twelve of them.

Sleeve choices are an easy way to bring lots of style to your dress without making a serious statement (as with a backless gown or a princess-style skirt). So, whether capped or Renaissance, sleeve style contributes greatly not only to the look of your gown but also to how you feel in it.

TOP: *A scoop backline paired with capped sleeves on this ball gown complements an upswept hairstyle and suits a bride with a flair for the dramatic.* BOTTOM: *These short, lacy, embroidered sleeves nicely complement the feminine neckline of this casually styled gown.*

Balloon		Just like they sound, balloon sleeves are short and puffy, on or off the shoulder. It's important that these sleeves are in proportion not only to the dress but also to your height and weight. Big sleeves can look festive, but they can quite easily look overdone.
Bell		These are long, full sleeves that are tapered down the arm and then flare at the wrist in the shape of a bell. Drawn out and elegant, these sleeves are often featured on medieval-style or Gothic dresses. They are a wonderful way to dress up a wedding gown for a winter wedding, because they don't add heft but nicely cover the arms.
Capped		A feminine, dainty look, capped sleeves are petite, fitted sleeves that just cap the top of the shoulder. These sleeves look best on sleek, toned upper arms.
Dolman		To produce a capelike effect, dolman sleeves extend from large armholes into a fitted wrist. This style was first seen in the Art Deco 1920s. The look is quite sophisticated and glamorous.
Bishop		Bishop sleeves are fuller in the forearm and gather at the wrist with a wide cuff. Not seen very often these days, this style was popular in the 1970s.

FAR LEFT: *These fitted illusion sleeves are stylish and chic with the addition of buttons and lace.*
LEFT: *See-through illusion sleeves are the perfect way to display your arms without baring them.*

Melon		Melon sleeves are a highly puffed, exaggerated form of Juliet sleeves that are rounded from the shoulder to just below the elbow. This look is perfect for theme weddings and more dramatic affairs.
Illusion		Illusion sleeves are made of illusion net and hug the contours of the arm. They are often adorned with beads or sequins. Illusion sleeves can be long or short and are a great way to show off skin without feeling naked. These sleeves make any gown look elegant and can work well at a nighttime wedding (they give a more formal look) or they can create a sexy look for a winter daytime affair (because they can be long but see-through). They can also work on a summer day, so the bride can stay cool but still look like she's covered up.
Juliet (or leg of mutton)		For the bride who has found her Romeo, Juliet sleeves may be just the thing. They puff out at the shoulder to just below the elbow, then are fitted to the wrist. This is a romantic sleeve that can be used perfectly on a gown as well as on a bridal coat.
Fitted		Just as they sound, fitted sleeves are sleek and hug the arm from shoulder to wrist. Your arms need to be in great shape to carry these sleeves off, because even though the skin is hidden, a lack of muscle tone will be completely visible.

TOP: *A boat-neck shell with three-quarter sleeves and princess seams is a simple, flattering choice for a bride, a bridesmaid, or any member of the wedding party.* BOTTOM: *This highly dramatic sleeve is a variation on the poet style. The peekaboo pleating adds a feminine sense of play.*

Poet

In the style of William Shakespeare, poet sleeves are full down to the wrist with ruffles or pleats at the end. This look is demure and sweet, just right for an autumn wedding or nighttime party.

Renaissance

With a slightly gathered puff at the shoulder that tapers down to just below the wrist, Renaissance sleeves are usually satin, with or without beads or sequins. These sleeves work well for all women and suit many dress styles.

Short

Slightly longer than capped sleeves, short sleeves are usually fitted sleeves that fall just before the midway point between the shoulder and the elbow. A more informal look, short sleeves work well on daytime dresses or at casual receptions.

Tapered

Tapered sleeves feature a slightly full, subtly gathered shoulder that tapers down to the wrist. The look adds some interest to long sleeves without being too dramatic or overdone.

Tulip

Short sleeves with two panels of fabric meet and overlap at the shoulder, creating a tulip shape. A more stylish version of the short sleeve, the tulip sleeve can dress up a daytime wedding gown.

Three-quarter

Three-quarter sleeves are fitted and end slightly below the elbow. A comfortable sleeve that covers the arm but doesn't restrict movement of the hands, the three-quarter sleeve looks good on almost everyone and allows you to wear bracelets more easily than with long sleeves.

TRAINS

Trains give an impression of opulence, formality, and wealth, and they never look appropriate at a casual reception. Whether you want to leave a lasting impression with your train by extending it the full length of the aisle or having its hemline end at your shoulders, you have a few different options. The important thing about trains is to consider not just how you want to look, but also whether there will be someone (or two) in your wedding party to help you deal with the abundance of fabric. The train must follow you down the aisle as smoothly as you're able to glide.

By the way, if you're looking to wear the longest train possible, you'll have to aim for something that measures roughly 24 feet (7 m)—that's the longest train ever worn, and not surprisingly, it was carried off by the beautiful Princess Diana.

RIGHT: *This extraordinary train is made of ruffled lace and attached to a casually tied but fabulously draped bow. The blend of ease and sophistication makes for a beautiful design.*

Royal cathedral

For the bride who wants her train to span the length of the aisle, the royal cathedral is the longest of the trains and extends 10 feet (3 m) or more. It is suitable for princesses, as well as those who believe their weddings are major events.

Cathedral

Also known as the monarch train, the cathedral train is the most formal train, extending 6 to 8 feet (1.8 to 2.4 m) from the waist. A dramatic statement, the cathedral train can be drawn up or detached after the ceremony to enable the bride to dance.

Chapel

The chapel train is a more notable medium-length train that extends 3½ to 5 feet (1.1 m to 1.5 m) from the hemline. This allows the gown to look more formal, without being as dramatic as the cathedral train.

Court

A court train is a narrow, modest train that extends up to 3 feet (about 1 m) from the hem. A regal look (hence the name), the court train used to be seen on medieval dresses as well as on wedding gowns.

Sweep

Sweep trains are short and modest, and they may or may not reach the floor. They create a pleasing back-line for the dress, without adding too much formality to the wedding.

Watteau

Named for the painter who made them popular by depicting brides in them, the Watteau train attaches to the shoulders or the top of a strapless gown. Because this look is rarely seen, it's a great way for a bride to make a one-of-a-kind entrance without being overly theatrical.

unveiled

GOWN EMBELLISHMENTS

Some brides prefer the simple, chic look of a straight satin gown, and others want a little—or a lot—of glitter and glam. For the latter group, there are embellishments in countless cuts, sizes, colors, and patterns to add some sparkle to the look.

If you love the color, cut, and fabric of a gown but feel it's too plain, there are many ways to add some excitement to its design. Beads and other accoutrements can be added after a dress is finished to lend a final touch of beauty. And you can personalize the embellishments, directing the seamstress on how much to add and where.

Appliqués
Fabric cutouts that are sewn onto the dress to create a pattern, appliqués may or may not be adorned with beads, embroidery, or sequins.

Beads
Beads can be made from glass, crystal, pearls, metal, or gems, and they can create a pattern on an entire dress or add detail to sleeves, hems, or necklines. Beads are a tasteful way to add color to your gown with soft, muted shades of pink, lavender, gold, blue, silver, or green.

Embroidery
Stitching that embellishes the surface of the dress fabric, embroidery can take the shape of various flowers and designs. Sometimes embroidery covers a dress; other times it adds hints of detail here and there, such as on the bodice, the ends of the sleeves, or the hem of the skirt.

Jewels
If you want to dazzle your guests, jewels will add sparkle and shine. Whether real or costume, diamonds, rubies, sapphires, or emeralds will make you and your gown striking.

Lace
With its delicate touch, lace may cover the entire gown or decorate certain sections, such as the skirt, bodice, neckline, backline, or sleeves.

To keep your marriage brimming,
With love in the loving cup,
Whenever you're wrong, admit it;
Whenever you're right, shut up.

—Ogden Nash, "To Keep Your Marriage Brimming"

Although Lady Diana certainly wore one of the loveliest gowns in history, everyone who woke up to view the wedding (in the United States, the ceremony was televised at 3 A.M.) was shocked when she first stepped out in a wrinkled gown. The dress did not travel well—at least in a carriage!

So, appearances aside, you have to think about comfort as well as practicality. This thing is going to be giving you a major hug as you go through a pretty incredible range of emotions, so you'll want the hug to be a comfy one.

With that said, you'll want be informed and knowledgeable about fabrics when you go to get your gown. This is, of course, even more important if you're having your gown made for you (see page 94).

THE ABCs OF FABRIC

Although all wedding gown fabrics are stunning, they can create vastly different looks, ranging from light and airy to fancy and sophisticated to sensuous and sleek.

To choose the right fabric for you, therefore, you first have to understand just what it is you're looking at. Not just because of how it will look, but also because of how it will feel given the time of year you'll be taking the marital plunge.

So to help you at least get your feet wet, here's a guide (including weights, appearances, and personalities) to the different types of fabric you'll encounter in your shopping days ahead.

ABOVE TOP: *A see-through overlay can instantly change your look... and help keep you warm if the weather is cool.*
ABOVE BOTTOM: *An array of laces and fabrics perfect for wedding gowns.*
OPPOSITE: *Soft blues and deep pinks will blend beautifully with stark white eyelet lace or an ivory Chantilly.*

*L*aces

All laces are not the same—the flowers, patterns, and design of lace can be placed on net or on another type of material as an overlay, or it be used on its own. Lace was originally created to replace embroidery. Whereas an embroidered design can be used on only one piece of fabric, a piece of lace can be created and then used on various dresses. If the lace is large enough, it can be used as a shawl or veil.

Lace can look light and summery or heavy and warm. It can be used on top of other fabric or worn on its own to allow the skin to be seen. If you find a dress that you like and it has some lace that you don't like, you can ask whether the lace can be changed. If you have antique lace or an antique dress with lace, you can also use that on a newly created dress.

Lace always look feminine and is common on a majority of wedding gowns for its sense of formality. A fabric store, seamstress's studio, or wedding gown salon will have the various choices for lace on display.

Alençon lace

As its name implies, this is an exquisite French lace with a delicate arrangement of flowers and heavy cording on a fine net background. It is very sophisticated, yet sexy at the same time.

All-over lace

This is a lace with a wide pattern that repeats over the entire expanse of the fabric. A dress can be made with all-over lace in patterns ranging from flowers to geometric designs.

Chantilly lace

This is a French lace with a graceful, delicate floral display and intertwining ribbons on a plain mesh background. It's usually edged with a finer, less defined cord than Alençon lace, which tends to give it a softer and more draping appearance.

Cluny lace

This is best described as an "old-fashioned" looking lace made of a loosely twisted yarn that gives it a thick, three-dimensional feel.

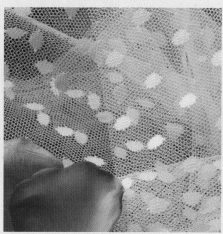

Coin-dot lace

This is a lace with circles or dots woven into the background netting.

Eyelet lace

Also called open-weave embroidery, this lace is characterized by its pattern of small, asymmetrical holes.

Reembroidered lace

This is simply a floral-patterned lace outlined with a border of cord.

Schiffli lace

This is a very lightweight, delicately embroidered floral lace that features cotton or rayon yarn embroidered onto a soft, sheer fabric, usually consisting of organza or polynet.

Venice lace

Venice is a very popular wedding dress fabric with a heavy raised floral design that, like Cluny lace, gives it a rich, three-dimensional appearance and feel.

Silk

Made from silkworm cocoons, silk is used in many wedding gown fabrics, including duchesse, Mikado, and shantung.

Laser cut silk

This is a modern silk that is cut with lasers to create amazingly intricate floral patterns.

Silk duchesse

Silk duchesse

This is very similar to duchess satin, but with a heavier, richer feel.

Silk shantung

Silk shantung

This is another silk with a thick and nubby texture, but it differs from silk dupioni in that its "nubs" are more randomly spaced.

Silk dupioni

Silk dupioni

Sounds like something you might get at a good Italian restaurant, but it's actually a thick and nubby silk, which looks rich but that is not as smooth as other silks.

Silk Mikado

A sleek and subtle silk, this fabric creates a sort of old-fashioned colonial look.

Taffeta

From the word taftan, which means to spin or twist (note its similarity to the word taffy), taffeta is a crisp (sorry, not chewy) fabric with a papery texture known to give it a rustling sound. It is used for linings as well as outer portions of gowns, and it comes in a shiny or matte finish.

Moiré taffeta

This is a taffeta with a distinctive watermarked, jagged-striped pattern. Moiré taffeta catches the light in a different way each time, creating an iridescent effect.

Moiré taffeta

Satin

This fashion stalwart is a shiny, dense, and opaque treatment of silk, with a smooth and lustrous sheen on one side and a matte finish on the other. The weight and drape of satin make it great for skirts of all lengths.

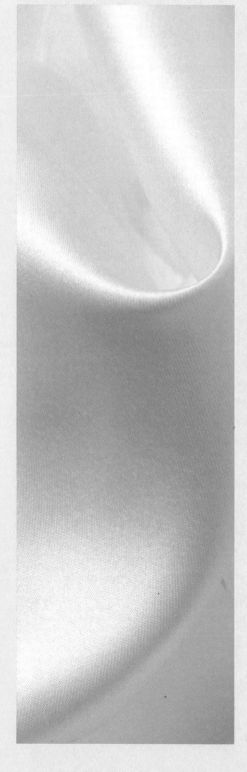

Peau de soie

Peau de soie

Translated from French, it means "skin of silk." This is a smooth, heavy-weight satin woven with an exquisitely fine ribbing. The dull luster is more flattering to most body shapes and sizes than high-luster satins. Polyester delustered satin is more forgiving than silk satins.

Slipper satin

Duchess satin

Duchess satin

Lighter than traditional satin, this fabric is an opulent blend of silk and rayon that is a good choice for warm-weather weddings because of its ability to hold its shape even after a length of time on the dance floor.

Italian satin

This is a heavier satin with lots of body that features a sophisticated, antique finish.

Slipper satin

This satin is especially soft and so shiny that it practically glows in the dark, which can be especially fun once the lights are low in the marital suite.

Brocade

Chiffon

Dotted Swiss

Brocade

This is a thick and rather heavy three-dimensional fabric embroidered with interwoven, raised designs and a satin-weave background that creates an artistic motif. Jackets or bodices are often made from brocade. This fabric is formal looking and quite traditional (it is also used in home décor).

Charmeuse

From the French word for "enchantress," charmeuse is a soft, lightweight satin woven from silk or rayon that has a modest sheen with the look and feel of whipped cream. Because of its subdued luster, charmeuse is often used in sheath or column dresses. It looks elegant without appearing heavy.

Chiffon

Also appetizingly light, billowy, and delicate, this is a sheer fabric with a simple weave, capable of making your walk down the isle feel like a magic carpet ride. Chiffon can be made from silk, polyester, or rayon and is often part of attendant and mother-of-the bride dresses.

Damask

Slightly lighter in weight than brocade, damask is a type of silk woven in floral or geometric patterns. The patterns are more subtle than those in a brocade, so the effect is more ethereal and understated than traditional.

Dotted Swiss

Sounds cheesy, we know, but dotted Swiss is a sheer, lightweight fabric embellished with small raised dots that can feel as good as they look. This fabric is great for summer ceremonies, casual weddings, and flower-girl dresses. It is not that common on wedding gowns.

Georgette

This sheer, lightweight fabric is often made of silk or polyester. It is slightly heavier and more opaque than chiffon. The twisted crepe fibers give it a springy quality that makes it seem to move on its own.

Jersey

Not just the Boss's home state, jersey is a stretchy fabric great for dresses designed to fit as snugly as a coat of paint. Jersey can include various percentages of cotton or Lycra, allowing for a more natural feel or a more synthetic stretch.

> **JUST SAY NO TO WRINKLES**
> As I said earlier, Princess Di's gorgeous gown was slightly ruined by its very apparent wrinkles. The key to ensuring your gown doesn't wrinkle is to give it the proper underlining. Make sure you tell the salespeople where you will be dressing and how you plan to get to the ceremony and reception. Even the most beautiful dress will suffer if it can't be treated properly on the big day. Let the schedule of your day (Long outdoor photo session? Long limousine ride to the church?) help you decide which fabric will work best for your gown. Remember, many gown styles can be made with different fabrics that are more appropriate for a hectic schedule or a change in the weather.

Organza

Organza

This is a crisp and transparent lighter-weight fabric similar to chiffon, with a muted luster that gives it a more formal look. It is made of silk, rayon, nylon, or polyester. In silk, the stiffness comes from the natural gum that remains on the fibers after processing. With man-made fibers the stiffness is engineered. In bridal gowns with an overskirt, organza is a beautiful choice, having just enough body to stand out yet still move nicely. In bridal gowns that have large puffy sleeves, an interlining of organza will hold the shape without adding bulk. It is also used as an interfacing where sheerness is a factor.

Tulle

Tulle

Used often for veils but also suitable for bodices or skirts, this is a netted fabric that comes in different grades, or weights. It can be used in heavy volume (such as for a large skirt or petticoat) or as one sheer layer.

Wool/silk

As the combination implies, this is a heavier fabric with a sensuously subtle sheen, great for winter weddings or churches with heating systems on the blink.

ONE WOMAN'S STORY
I work at a catering company in Philadelphia and am catering a wedding this April for a woman who is getting married in Switzerland in an ice cave. The bride and groom are being carried up the mountain in a carriage and then are going to get out and stand inside the ice cave to be married by a judge. The bride is going to wear white go-go boots, a white knee length dress with a white faux fur coat and top hat. If that isn't original I don't know what is. I think it's wonderful!

–Carmel Cantiello, Pennsylvania

WHO WORE WHITE?
The first known white wedding dress was worn in 1499 by Anne of Brittany, for her marriage to Louis XII of France. Until that time, women simply wore their best dress, often yellow or red in color. In biblical times, most dresses were blue because blue symbolized purity.

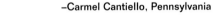

Perfect for the classic bride, this strapless gown is tasteful and timeless.

THE SPECTRUM OF WHITES

Once you've shopped for a wedding gown, you'll never look at white the same way again. Many women who are first-time wedding gown shoppers think they'll need to choose simply "white" or "cream," only to spend days realizing all the options in between. The game just begins when you decide that your gown will be "white." Then you'll also need to consider "stark" or "bright" white, "natural" white, ivory, cream, ecru, diamond, candlelight, champagne, gold, and (I love this one) nude.

More confusing yet, every company has its own interpretation of these colors, so there's no standard for reference. The ivory at David's Bridal may look a lot different from the ivory at your neighborhood shop.

The best way to pick a shade of white is to get a swatch of the fabric you like most and take it outside and to various places with different types of light and hold it against your skin. Does it bring out the whites of your eyes and make your skin look healthy? Or does it give you a pallor or drain you of color? If you worry that you've never looked good in white, have no fear; like skin, white can have blue or yellow undertones, and that will determine which one flatters you best.

If you do decide to opt for a dress within the rainbow of whites, it's imperative that you choose the best shade of white for your particular skin tone. If you fall into the summer or winter seasons in terms of your coloring (see page 57), you'll look best in a stark or

bright white dress. If you're more of a spring or autumn hue, on the other hand, you'll look most radiant in a dress that's an off-white or creamy shade.

A RAINBOW OF COLORS

Although most brides still opt for traditional white gowns on their wedding day, some are more adventurous and choose a dress with some color to give it a little more … attitude. It's all one big green light when it comes to color, with some brides now sauntering down the aisle in even the most unusual of sky blues.

Playing it safe, however, the bridal industry has been catering to this "anything goes" attitude gradually, offering color options as accents more so than as hues for the entire gown. You could consider a blue ribbon band across the bodice of a strapless dress that drapes down into a train, for example, or a white dress adorned with amethyst, blue, or rose quartz crystals. Or how about a white dress decorated with blue, pink, and yellow ribbons in the shapes of flowers?

For the bride who wants to wear one solid color, pastels are now popular, particularly shades of pink. And when we say pink, we mean a pink that can vary from just a pinch

LEFT: *This ornate, colorfully embroidered bodice is sure to make an impression.*
OPPOSITE: *To the untrained eye, these gowns all look "white." Look more closely, and you'll discover they are a rainbow of whites—all distinctly different shades.*

to a fistful of tint. There is also a wide variety of blues and faint turquoise shades out there. You might consider a gold dress with metallic threading to make for a dramatic in-your-face look? Some brides are even opting to walk down the aisle in a black or—heaven forbid—red dress, which is sure to have grandma gasping.

As you can see, deciding on a wedding dress is a bit more like rocket science and brain surgery than many of us realize. So to make your choice a wise one, don't be afraid to talk with a bridal consultant. Many of these experts can tell the minute they see you whether you'd be more stunning in pink chiffon or Chantilly lace, and they'll steer you in the right direction.

ABOVE: *This deep burgundy strapless bridesmaid's gown is perfect for a colder season or evening wedding.*

LEFT: *This modish soft pink gown coupled with long gloves and a stylish faux pink fur creates a chic, wintry look.*

FIT THE TIME OF YEAR

In these "anything goes" days, you can pretty much wear any fabric you choose at any time of the year. But for maximum elegance and comfort, you may want to opt for a lighter, airier fabric in a warmer month and a heavier fabric when there's a nip in the air.

Some fabrics—such as tulle, for example—can be worn at any time of the year. Tulle is great for a June wedding because it's light and netted, and it also can give you a special, princess feel for a Christmas wedding.

A recent trend, demonstrated more and more frequently by Vera Wang, is to mix fabric weights, such as a thin silk chiffon gown matched with a wool throw. Keep up to date on how designers are experimenting, and your options will multiply.

unveiled
IF YOU'RE NOT WEARING WHITE

If you do choose to go with a wedding dress that makes a statement with its color, it's still a good idea to select a shade that complements your skin tone, hair, and eyes.

■ ABOVE: *Tuned into her "spring" hair and skin coloring, this bride chose flattering mint fabric over white.*

you're a "spring" if

↬ **Your skin is peach, beige, golden beige, or ivory with freckles**

↬ **Your hair is golden, flaxen blond, strawberry blond, red, auburn, or golden brown**

↬ **Your eyes are clear blue, deep blue, golden green, clear green, teal, light golden brown, or hazel**

Think Marilyn Monroe or Gwen Stefani!

Colors to consider: shades of teal, warm pinks, periwinkle, camel, golden brown

you're an "autumn" if

↬ **Your skin is ivory beige, light beige (sometimes with freckles), peach, bronze, or golden beige**

↬ **Your hair is honey blonde, red, chestnut brown, copper, charcoal black, or dark brown with reddish highlights**

↬ **Your eyes are clear green, golden, avocado green, reddish brown, hazel, or teal**

Think Nicole Kidman or Tyra Banks!

Colors to consider: warm greens, gold, almond, ivory, peach

you're a "summer" if

↬ **Your skin is porcelain, pinkish, rosy beige (tans easily), or beige with a hint of yellow**

↬ **Your hair is ash, gray-blond, ash brown, dark brown, or brown with auburn highlights**

↬ **Your eyes are icy blue, dark blue, aqua, gray blue, gray green, clear green, hazel, soft brown, or gray brown**

Think Heidi Klum or Kate Winslet!

Colors to consider: cool shades of pink, mauve, slate blue, lavender

you're a "winter" if

↬ **Your skin is copper, beige, dark brown, honey brown, or olive**

↬ **Your hair is medium brown, dark brown, black, blue-black, or chestnut**

↬ **Your eyes are hazel, brown, or dark brown**

Think Lucy Liu or Liz Taylor!

Colors to consider: strong, vivid shades of red and blue, jewel tones, black

4 FLATTERING YOUR SHAPE
the best style for your body type

"My most brilliant achievement was my ability to be able to persuade my wife to marry me."

—*Winston Churchill*

It's not really about the dress. It's really about you and the dress. The dress and you have a relationship. It might look fabulous on the hanger but not flatter your best features. It might hang awkwardly in the store, but come alive as soon as you put it on. One key to finding the perfect gown is knowing which styles look best on your particular body.

You want a dress that will make you look well proportioned and will tastefully accentuate your best assets. There are four basic body shapes, and you fit into one of them whether you're 5' 2" or 6' 3" (157 cm or 185 cm).

the pear	A pear-shaped woman has narrow shoulders and wider hips. Pears usually have a two-size difference between their top and bottom. For example, if you're a size ten on the top and a size twelve on the bottom then you're a pear.
the inverted triangle	If you have broad shoulders and narrower hips, you're an inverted triangle. Inverted triangles often have a full bust and yet wear a smaller-sized pant.
the rectangle	If your shoulders, hips, and waist are all pretty much the same width, then you're a rectangle. Sometimes, rectangles are considered to have a "boyish figure."
the hourglass	If your hips and bust are the same size, and you have a defined waist, then you're an hourglass.

ABOVE: *This spaghetti-strapped sheath is a wonderful choice for a slender bride.*
OPPOSITE: *Strapless gowns are graceful and elegant, and can make a bride appear polished and refined.*

CHOOSING THE RIGHT STYLE DRESS FOR YOUR BODY

The secret to finding the best gown for your body type is to find one that will draw attention to your best features and deemphasize your less than perfect ones. In a sense, you want to create an optical illusion with your gown.

Here are some guidelines for each body type:

the pear

Your goal is to add width to the upper part of your body and deemphasize your lower half. A portrait collar, capped sleeves, or beading on the top of the dress, combined with a simple lower half, will do the trick.

The best dress style for the pear is an A-line or princess cut that moves with your body shape without being too clingy. A higher waistline will also deemphasize your hips and make you appear more slender.

Other good choices include dresses with diagonal bands across the bodice, shirred bodices, wide necklines, jeweled or ruffled necklines, and off-the-shoulder styles.

What not to do Don't choose a style that will add any weight to your bottom half. You don't want heavy folds in the dress, a full skirt, or bustles or bows in the back. And avoid detailing on the skirt, such as beads or sequins, which will draw the eye there. Dresses that hug the body, such as sheaths or mermaid styles, also will accentuate the pear shape.

On the top of your dress, steer clear of high or halter necklines that will bring the eye inward and make your shoulders look narrow.

LEFT: *The simple, graceful lines of this dress flatter a pear-shaped figure.*

the wedding gown book

the inverted triangle

You're the opposite shape of the pear, so you want to deemphasize your top and draw attention to your bottom half. The inverted triangle should choose a dress with a very simple top and some kind of texture, such as beads, crystals, sequins, or lace, on the skirt.

Also look for gowns with an elongated bodice that will draw the eye down and lengthen your upper body. Dresses with a dropped U- or V-shaped waist (called a Basque) or belted dresses will flatter your hips and create a waistline. Ideal sleeves for an inverted triangle are simple with minor gathers that follow the natural shoulder line.

What not to do Don't accentuate your top. Some women who are top-heavy feel the need to feature it with a low-cut dress, but you should really be modest on top on your wedding day. Stay away from dresses that are textured on top with beads, lace, or sequins. Also avoid oversized sleeves with elaborate detailing, straight skirts, or empire-style dresses—all will accentuate top-heaviness.

RIGHT: *Basque waistlines with lightly adorned necklines draw attention away from an inverted triangle's torso.*

the rectangle

If you wish, you can wear more of a sleek, sophisticated dress that doesn't have a definite shape. If you'd rather give the illusion of curves, you can also choose a princess-style dress to give some definition to your waist and hips. Or, an empire-style dress will camouflage your waist and place emphasis on your bodice and hemlines. Another option is to wear a jacket over your dress that adds some detail to your waistline.

What not to do Don't choose a dress style that has a definite dart, such as a bustline you need to fill.

LEFT: *An empire waist is accentuated by a sheer Watteau train and an open back.*

the hourglass

Most wedding gowns are cut in an hourglass shape, so of all the body types you'll have the easiest time finding a dress. You can pretty much do whatever you want in a wedding gown, as long as your top half doesn't look too full. If you want to accentuate your curves, you may opt for a sheath dress or a mermaid style. Basque or dropped waistlines will help emphasize your natural waist. If you'd rather look a little less curvy, choose a simple dress with classic lines—nothing puffy or detailed. An A-line, princess style, or an off-the-shoulder dress, will also flatter you.

What not to do Your only restriction is you don't want your top or bottom half to look too full. Avoid very low V-necks or heavy bodice or skirt detailing, which can make you appear heavier overall.

RIGHT: *A lace overlay on the bodice adds just a hint of lavishness to this simple dress.*

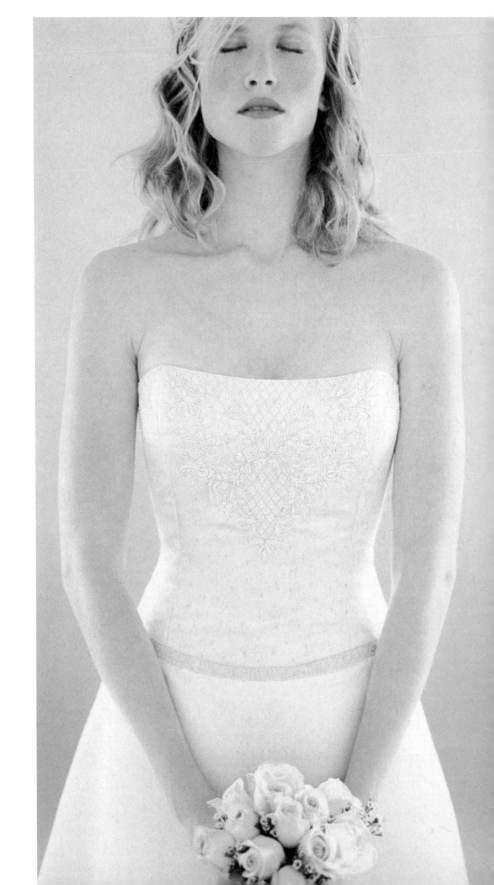

ABOVE: *A bustled skirt or textured train can help balance out a large bust.*

OTHER FIGURE CONSIDERATIONS

Choosing the best style for your body type is only half the battle. The dress also has to fit well and flatter you at every angle. Remember: Even the best photographer won't be able to catch your "best side" every time. So make sure your dress looks great in the front, back, and on the sides by checking it out thoroughly in a full-length, three-sided mirror.

While the following problems may sound mundane, they can look unattractive on your wedding day. Take the time to look for fat hanging over the back of your dress; excessive cleavage; too many moles, freckles, or birthmarks on your back; and sleeves that squeeze your arms and make them look flabby.

Beyond the four basic body types, there are a few other body-specific elements you'll want to consider when choosing your dress.

If you're plus sized	Less is more. If you're going to wear a dress with beads or crystals, keep them subdued and choose the flat rather than rounded ones. Also stay away from dresses that are too fitted or clingy.
If you're petite	A petite woman should not let her dress overwhelm her. You want people to notice you, not the dress. If you're smaller than 5'4", stay away from big, puffy dresses. Instead, opt for something slim, simple, and form fitting, which will make you look taller.
If you're tall	On a tall woman, the most common dress styles can appear too high waisted. To avoid this problem, choose an already high-cut princess or empire waist.
If you have a large bust	Go for a simple top that gives you more coverage and is not accentuated with beads, sequins, or lace.
If you have a small bust	Add weight to your top with sequins or beads. A square neckline or spaghetti straps will be flattering.
If your arms are on the bigger side	You don't want a strapless dress or a dress with capped sleeves. Long or three-quarter sleeves will flatter you best.

Finally, while your tattoo may look fabulous peeking out from a tank top or hip huggers, you might not want to see just a piece of it in the photographs of your wedding day. Distractions become the focus of everyone's attention for the rest of the night, and they may rob the bride of the attention of her guests.

unveiled

BOOST YOUR BODY IMAGE AND FEEL LIKE A PRINCESS

Someone has fallen in love with you and asked to share his life with you, and yet rather than focusing on the life that is ahead, all you can think about is how you want to lose weight before your wedding. Body image is an issue almost all women struggle with, and it's important to remember that how you feel about yourself has very little to do with how you really look to others.

For a woman with a poor body image, trying on wedding gowns can be a harrowing exercise in self-hatred. And an upcoming wedding can turn that woman to crash dieting and excessive exercise, which can, in turn, lead to poor nutrition, injuries, and depression.

Don't expect to feel better about yourself just because you're getting married. Validation that comes from the outside is not what someone with a poor body image needs. You need to feel good about yourself no matter what your weight or your relationship status.

Lots of women focus on losing weight for their wedding, but here are some healthful ideas that will not only help you look good, but will also, more importantly, help you feel good on this most special day.

꙳ **Don't bring your most critical friend with you to look for a dress. Instead, bring your most loving, supportive friends who focus not on exteriors, but on the person you are.**

꙳ **Eat to feel good on the big day, not to feel thin. Strive not for a number on the scale but for a weight at which you feel strong and energetic. Ask yourself whether your diet contributes—or takes away from —your health and energy level.**

꙳ **Think about the things you want to do on your honeymoon, not how you want to look in a bikini. Regular exercise creates power and endurance, which can help you enjoy more activities. Can you hike as far as you want to? Would you like to try kayaking? Exercising for an activity rather than for the way you look is more likely to keep you fit and healthy.**

꙳ **Finally, remember that if you feel your body image has become a preoccupation, don't hesitate to talk to a counselor or therapist. Remember, beauty really does come from within—and chances are your fiancé, your friends, and your family see your beauty even if you can't. If you catch yourself feeling bad that you're wearing a size 12 gown rather than a size 6, don't let that negative voice suck you in. Follow it with 10 positive thoughts, and let someone know how you feel. A good friend or a counselor—or, in the best of all worlds, your future husband—will help you see that you are gorgeous just as you are right now.**

▪ ABOVE: *Your wedding day is a time to celebrate and accentuate your strengths.*

5 *FLATTERING YOUR DISPOSITION*

the best style for your personality

"There is something about a wedding gown prettier than any other gown in the world."

—Douglas Jerrod, 1859

ABOVE: *If you've always dreamed of looking like a princess on your wedding day, a full skirt help complete the look.*
OPPOSITE: *The gown you choose should match your personality. This dress is fun, feminine, and fabulous.*

Your wedding day will give you the unique opportunity to communicate something very special about yourself to some very special people, so you want to get it right. All the choices you make, from the church to the reception hall to the flowers, will create the backdrop and set the tone for the two things your guests will pay attention to most: you and your gown.

So before you even begin to think about calling a reception hall or selecting your wedding colors, take a good, honest look at yourself and try to determine what we might call your wedding "personality." This personality will help guide you through all the potentially mind-boggling choices you'll need to make.

If you're like most women, your wedding persona will pretty closely match the persona that gets you through an average day. If you're laid-back you'll probably be happier with a smaller, more casual affair. But if you're more of a demonstrative and romantic type, you may have a better time with some pomp and circumstance—and enough champagne to help it all go down. In either case, your gown, of course, will need to match.

Then again, you may want to seize your wedding day as a chance to reinvent yourself, to become someone you've always wanted to be rather than who you have been. This can be the first day of the rest of your life, after all, so for heaven's sake don't waste it.

THE FOUR WEDDING PERSONALITIES

There are billions of women in the world, and each of us has our own style. But for simplicity's sake, let's boil all of us down into just four basic types—romantic, natural, classic, and dramatic. In most cases, these styles will carry over to the choices we will make with respect to our wedding gowns. You probably have a good idea of which category you fit most snugly into, but if you're not sure, here's some help. (And please note that these categories are rough approximations at best. Most of us exhibit attributes of more than one.)

the hopeless romantic

You've been dreaming of your wedding day since you learned to walk, and you've got fairy-tale expectations. You picture yourself getting married in a church filled with flowers, or in a gazebo surrounded by a luscious garden. Your style of dress is typically feminine and frilly, with lots of dreamy and ethereal accesories, and shades of pink.

If this is you, know that you can make your wedding as formal or informal as you want, as long as it's dripping with romance. When choosing a gown, lean toward more feminine styles with lace and ruffles. To emulate the Cinderella look, you may want to go for a strapless bodice with a full skirt and a cathedral train and veil, complete with long gloves. Or you may want to select a lightweight, heavenly tulle dress, or perhaps a gown hand-painted with flowers. Some romantic brides go the historical route and wear a Renaissance or Edwardian-inspired style. As for brands, look for dresses by Justina McCaffrey, Michelle Roth, Amelia Casablanca, Daniel Thompson, Eve of Milady, Candice Solomon, Lazaro, and Louise Hamlin Wright.

TOP: *The romantic bride will choose a feminine gown with exquisite details, like this soft, flowing chiffon back.*
BOTTOM: *Corset bodices are figure flattering and theatric.*
OPPOSITE: *What could be more romantic than a Cinderella-inspired crisp white ball gown?*

the natural bride

You see your wedding in an outdoor setting—maybe the beach or the backyard of the house in which you grew up. And while you want to look your best, you also want to appear relaxed, simple, and pure. If it's not comfortable, you won't wear it—period! Your closet is full of jeans, T-shirts, and low-heeled shoes.

As the natural bride, therefore, a formal wedding is apt to make you very nervous, so think about a semiformal or informal occasion instead. For your gown, you'll probably feel best in a loose, simple, soft, and flowing dress with minimal embellishments. And because you value comfort, consider it essential that you put your prospective gown through all imaginable movements before you buy. Dance, hug, bend down, sit, and walk—do everything you foresee yourself doing on the big day to make sure the dress feels good and can hold up. For a garment capable of such a performance, consider dresses by Genny, Manolo, Amarildine, Christina, Couture, Elizabeth Fillmore, Amy Michelson, Amy Kuschel, Reva Mivasagar, and Rostarose.

BOTTOM LEFT: *The natural bride will gravitate toward an uncomplicated neckline, such as this pretty scoop.*
BOTTOM RIGHT: *These soft, flowing gowns are understated yet very stylish.*
OPPOSITE: *This simple, flowing gown is no frills—suited for the natural bride.*

the classic bride

You see the big day as being formal or semiformal and conservative, with lots of traditions from your mother, her mother, and your groom's family. Your dress style, therefore, should be refined, tasteful, and, above all, classy. It's a style you've liked all along, after all—timely and yet timeless. Perhaps a white, full-length gown with a fitted bodice, a court train, a subtle sprig of lace, and pearls would fill this bill best. So if you don't wind up dusting off such an outfit from your mother or grandmother, consider gowns by Jenny Lee, Dessy Diamond, Anne Barge, Alvina Valente, Amelia Carrara, Christos, Jim Hjelm, Peter Langner, Richard Glassgow, Amsale, and Ron LoVese.

TOP: *Classic brides are likely to prefer full length gowns with traditional, refined cuts and lines.*
OPPOSITE: *This breathtaking two-piece gown is elegant and striking.*

ONE WOMAN'S STORY

I was married in 1989 to a man who is Navajo. I'm Jewish, from Brooklyn. It was very important to my husband that we get married in a Navajo ceremony, and so that's just what we did. My entire family flew to New Mexico, and my husband's grandfather, a medicine man, married us in a hogan, the traditional Navajo dwelling.

My mother-in-law told me that I would wear a velveteen skirt and blouse, which she would make for me. I got to pick the color, a beautiful deep blue. And when we got to the Four Corners, I had to buy moccasins to wear with the outfit. On the morning of the wedding, my in-laws brought stunning silver jewelry for me to wear with the dress.

The ceremony was beautiful and it meant a lot to me that I was able to give my husband the wedding that he wanted. But it always bothered me that I never got to wear the white dress, because that was the tradition I grew up in.

—Donna Raskin, Massachusetts

the drama queen

In your mind's eye your wedding is an elegant affair, held in the evening, with lots of candlelight and five-star food. Your style of dress is avant-garde, eclectic, and stylish, and you like to be noticed... a lot. You've always got the latest fashions in your closet, and you're not afraid to take a risk when you dress. And your risks usually pay off.

So your dress? Because you're more daring you'll want a gown with some punch. You may opt for an elegant, strapless and backless, full-length mermaid sheath. Or you may choose to draw attention with elaborate sequins, beading, or color. You also may choose to sport a fabulous new hairstyle or hat. But no matter what you choose, it will be creative, so to help you in that choice, look for gowns by Ines Di Santo, Ian Stewart, Beverly Summers, Eva Hayna Forsythe, and Guzzo.

Now that you've examined your wedding gown personality, you can begin to build your backdrop. Before you set foot in a bridal salon, you should have your church and reception hall booked. This will allow you to coordinate the shade and style of your dress with the places it will be seen and photographed. Bottom line? You have a ton of challenging but very fun and exciting decisions ahead of you.

TOP: *The dramatic can border on unusual, like this fur head-piece coupled with the ultrashiny satin gown.*

FAR RIGHT: *Drama can also be expressed in the cut of a gown, such as with this form-fitting mermaid style.*

RIGHT: *Extra fabric and adornments can add drama, such as this chiffon Watteau train.*

OPPOSITE: *The elaborate beading on the top of this show-stopping gown gives it the added pizzazz the dramatic bride seeks.*

unveiled

PERFECT FITS

So which prominent figures might represent not just the four most basic wedding personalities mentioned above but also some additional subcategories you could identify with? Let's play paparazzi and see whose privacy we can invade to find out.

the romantic bride

Princess Diana. She emerged from a horse-drawn carriage in an ivory taffeta gown trimmed with bows, pearls, sequins, antique lace...and a 25-foot-long (7.6 m) train!

the natural bride

Cindy Crawford. When Cindy married Randy Gerber in 1998, she chose to tie the knot ocean-side in the Bahamas, wearing a short, white, slip-style dress with a simple veil and a single flower in her hair.

the classic bride

Grace Kelly. When saying "I do" to Prince Ranier III of Monaco, Kelly wore a classic wedding gown created from silk taffeta and antique lace, a Welsh tulle veil, and a Greco-Roman–style headpiece with flowers made of even more silk.

the dramatic bride

Gwen Stefani. Gwen exchanged vows with Gavin Rossdale, the British musician and front man for Bush, wearing a bright pink-and-white silk faille custom-made by John Galliano for Christian Dior.

the versatile bride

Sarah Michelle Gellar. When marrying Freddie Prinze, Jr. in an outdoor ceremony, Sarah wore a strapless Vera Wang with terry-cloth Mella thongs, changing after the ceremony into a decidedly more fun-loving BCBG frock.

the cozy bride

Kate Hudson. To make it official with Black Crows' lead singer Chris Robinson, Kate got married at night and went with a winter theme, wearing white boots and a flurry-inspired gown with long, arm-warming sleeves.

LEFT: *Soft pink shades are a wonderful way to add color without straying too far from tradition.*

WHAT'S YOUR WEDDING GOWN PERSONALITY?

If you're not sure which wedding gown personality best fits you, take the following quiz. You might learn a thing or two about yourself.

Your favorite flower is:
a. Orchid
b. Daisy
c. Rose
d. Hydrangea

Your favorite alcoholic drink is:
a. Martini
b. Beer
c. Champagne
d. Red wine

Your preferred hairstyle is:
a. It doesn't matter, as long as it's the latest style
b. Any way, as long as I don't have to spend much time on it
c. Long and flowing or in ringlet curls
d. Well-coiffed and sophisticated style

Your preferred style of makeup is:
a. Noticeable, with lots of sparkle
b. What makeup?
c. Lots of pink and blush tones
d. Tasteful and refined

When you go out on the town, you usually wear:
a. Something sequined, beaded, brightly colored, or low-cut
b. Jeans and a comfortable shirt
c. A flowing skirt or dress
d. Black pants and a tailored shirt

Your favorite way to spend a Saturday is:
a. Shopping in the city, followed by a night out
b. Biking, hiking, or any other outdoor activity
c. Being with your fiancé on a romantic picnic
d. Picking out home decor

The thing that most attracted you to your fiancé was:
a. His dynamic, unpredictable personality
b. His love of the outdoors
c. The way he professed his love
d. His sensibility

scoring

If you picked mostly A's:
You're dramatic. Go for a dress with lots of fireworks, such as sparkles, sequins, and beading.

If you picked mostly B's:
You're a natural. Shop for a dress that's comfortable, understated, and, above all, simple.

If you picked mostly C's:
You're romantic. You'll feel most like yourself in a gown with lots of ruffles or lace.

If you picked mostly D's:
You're a classic. You will look and feel best in a tasteful, elegant gown that achieves dignity with its tailored lines.

"Bridesmaids may soon be brides; one wedding brings on another."

–C.H. Spurgeon, Salt-cellars (1919)

This may be the only time in your life you can appropriately tell your closest friends and family what to wear. Styling the attendants in your wedding will be tons of fun and undeniably challenging at the same time. If you're like most brides, you've probably got a wide array of body sizes, personalities, and fashion senses to juggle. But remember: It's your wedding, and it's all up to you. The most important thing is that you're happy with the gowns and tuxedos your attendants wear. And because your friends and family respect you and your taste, they're bound to love what you choose for them.

Like your wedding gown, the fabrics, styles, and colors you select for your attendants will be determined in part by the weather, the level of formality, and the theme of your wedding.

DRESSING THE BRIDESMAIDS

Inviting women to be members of your bridal party dates back to ancient times. One Roman custom was to dress the bridesmaids in a fashion similar to that of the bride to confuse evil spirits who might try to kidnap the bride. Bridesmaids also had the role of fending off unsuitable suitors, leaving the bride for her groom. Although the specific functions of being a bridesmaid have changed over time, being the bride's support system, confidante, defender, and friend hasn't.

Consider yourself—and your bridesmaids—lucky. For years, bridesmaids stuffed puffy, garish gowns in the back of their closets after a wedding, knowing full well they'd never wear them again. But today, bridesmaids' dresses have stepped out of the taffeta cookie cutter and into fashion. So much so, in fact, that your bridesmaids will be making up reasons to wear their gowns again.

TOP: *This calf-length A-line cut will look wonderful on all the bridesmaids' figures.*
BOTTOM: *A sample swatch from a bridesmaid's dress.*
OPPOSITE: *Bridesmaids dresses are no longer made to be pushed to the back of the closet after the big day. Today's dresses are stylish, trendy, and very versatile.*

Rules for bridesmaids' dresses have relaxed. You can even choose something off the rack at your local department store if you want (just be careful you don't pick a dress one of your guests may also be wearing). There are a few general rules you can follow:

Same color, same gown	If your wedding is on the formal side, or you just want to be fair, you can choose the same gown for all your bridesmaids. And it's easy—one decision and you're done. The downside is this: As you learned in the flattering your figure chapter, not all body types look stunning in all dresses. So if you decide to go this route, you may want to choose a style that looks wonderful on most body types, such as an A-line or princess cut.
Same gown, different colors	Let's face it—not everyone looks good in melon. For extra flavor, and to make sure each one of your bridesmaids is wearing her best shade, you can choose one dress style and pick a specific color for each attendant, and then merge the colors together with your flowers. One potential negative to this approach is that unless you pick extremely tasteful, complementing colors, things may start to look a little busy during the ceremony. And there's always the chance that one woman may decide she likes another woman's color better and become resentful (petty, but possible).
Same color, different gowns	Many brides are opting to go this route because it's a happy medium between a monochromatic, formal look and a bridal rainbow. There are a few ways you can approach this. You can be extra hands-off and allow your bridesmaids to pick their own gown as long as it is black, red, or whichever color you choose. Or you can work with a bridal shop to pick out a few different styles in the same color (full dresses, skirt and top pieces, or both), and either let your bridesmaids pick their favorites or help them choose their styles. For example, in one color, a store may offer eight different tops in three different fabrics that can be matched with four different skirts.

TOP: *Because your bridesmaids are sure to have different skin tones, it's a good idea to choose a color that flatters most, such as this navy.* BOTTOM: *This fun, asymmetrical, raspberry gown is appropriate for any season.*

Choosing separates that are the same color but a different style is a great way to maintain a uniform look while still giving your brides- maids a few options.

In terms of color, I dare you to try to find a shade that hasn't been used for a bridesmaid's dress. Some of the more progressive colors include black (even black lace!), chocolate brown, and iridescent fabrics that illuminate different spectrums depending on the lighting.

Tasteful splashes of beadwork, crystals, and sequins are becoming more and more popular on bridesmaids' dresses, as are patterned dresses or patterned skirts paired with solid tops. A solid-colored, simple gown decorated with a single ribbon around the waist is a classic look, as are shorter and more fitted gowns. And if one of your bridesmaids is expecting, there are plenty of stylish maternity bridesmaids' gowns out there as well.

■ ABOVE: *One of your bridesmaids is expecting? No problem—there are many stylish options out there for the bridesmaid mother-to-be.*
RIGHT: *For an outdoor garden wedding, consider a natural flowing floral dress, like this one.*
OPPOSITE LEFT: *To bring a subtle rainbow of color to your wedding party, choose an iridescent shade, like this periwinkle blue.*
OPPOSITE FAR LEFT: *This decorated strapless bridesmaid dress is adorable, creative, and fun.*

In general, the rules are: the more formal the wedding and the cooler the season, the darker the bridesmaids' dresses and the heavier the fabric. For instance, for an evening wedding around the holiday season, you may want to choose a velvet, silk brocade, or duchess satin in a darker shade, such as navy, dark red, deep purple, or black. Or for a summer wedding outside, a lighter shade, such as pink, pale green, or soft lavender in a fabric such as charmeuse or chiffon may look best. But of course, rules were meant to be broken, so by no means do you have to follow them.

ONE WOMAN'S STORY

You have to understand, we don't know where my sister came from. My parents got married in Vegas, my brother got hitched on a sailboat, my husband and I eloped in Gibraltar when I was 19, but my sister Kim was different. As a publicist in Manhattan and the proud owner of eight Jimmy Choos and six Manolo Blaniks, Kim wouldn't strike you as the most down to earth person you've ever encountered. I suppose it should have come as no surprise to me that when it was time for her to tie the knot she turned into Bridezilla; the statistics were dizzying: seven bridesmaids, two junior brides- maids, three hundred guests; glass swans, ice sculptures, taffeta, lace, Jordan almonds; my bridesmaid dress made me look like the lining of a swimming pool! Who would have guessed that the seamstress who completely botched my sister's gown would have helped me see the deeper side of my sister? When Kim got the news she reacted as expected, bursting into tears, mascara running down her face; it took her fiancé's mother, Anne, three tries before her offer to give Kim her dress was actually heard. Anne is the mother of six boys, and had always prayed to have a daughter to pass her wedding gown to, so it tells you the kind of faith this woman has to hold onto that dress for so long. What really floored me was how selflessly Kim realized what it would mean to Anne to wear that dress; she looked her right in the eye and said she would be honored, and never shed a tear for her botched dress again. Anne's dress really was beautiful, though not quite my sister's style, making me all the proud- er to zip her into that thing. That fiasco made me realize that my sister, despite all of our differences, is a pretty cool lady and one that I totally admire.

–Niamh Sheedy, Dublin, Ireland

TOP: For a more casual affair, consider a fun, knee-length style for the bridesmaids.
BOTTOM: Dark shades— like this deep plum—give the ceremony a more formal feel.
OPPOSITE: This decorative beaded neckline adds style and sophistication to this striking dark blue gown.

ABOVE: *Handsome, polished, and coordinated groomsmen flank the affectionate couple at this seaside ceremony.*

DRESSING THE GROOM AND GROOMSMEN

Selecting the groom and groomsmen's attire doesn't leave nearly as much room for creative expression as does picking out the bridesmaids' dresses, but there are still some fun decisions to be made. Remember— half of the attendants will be guys, and you want them to look as spiffy as you and your girls will look gorgeous.

Many couples dress their groomsmen in one of their two or three wedding colors. If the colors are navy and silver, for instance, the guys will wear navy or silver vests. This becomes trickier when the colors are something like lavender and yellow, because getting the men to stroll down the aisle willingly in pale purple will most likely be a struggle at best. So in the case of pastels—or if you just want a simpler look—you may want to opt for a neutral metallic or earth color for your groomsmen, such as silver, gold, ivory, white, or gray.

As far as the tuxedo accessories are concerned, classic is the rule— gone are the ruffled jackets and shiny shoes (at least for now, thank goodness) and in is the long Fordham tie with a full-back vest and a longer-style jacket. But if your groomsmen prefer no vest, a shorter jacket, or a jacket with tails, those are all fine looks, too. Although the rules for tuxedos are stricter than those for dresses, they're still not hard and fast.

If you really want to get crazy—and your groomsmen are super agreeable—you can dress them in colored tuxedo jackets, such as maroon, red, or blue, with black pants. Or you can choose a patterned vest or tie. And when done right, colored shirts paired with the same color tie and cummerbund can be a tasteful, monochromatic look.

WEARING YOUR HEART ON YOUR SLEEVE

The groom is supposed to wear a flower in his lapel that appears in the bride's bouquet. This tradition "stems" from medieval times, when a knight wore his lady's colors as an outward declaration of his love for her.

unveiled

DRESSING THE REST OF YOUR ATTENDANTS

dressing the moms

In formal weddings, the mother of the bride and the mother of the groom usually wear elegant evening gowns or dressy suits, often in a shade that complements the wedding colors. Or the mother of the bride wears ivory or cream, while the mother of the groom wears an outfit of her choice. Attire for the mother of the bride and mother of the groom is available in bridal shops, or you can go for something from a department store or nonbridal boutique. Again, the rules are easily and often bent, so it's up to you, your mom, and your future mother-in-law to go for whatever you want.

dressing the kids

A surefire way to get extra ooohs and aaahs at your wedding is to include children in the ceremony. Whether it's a handsome young chap who bestows the ring, or a sweet little girl who strews rose petals down the aisle, kids are a charming touch, especially when they're dressed to the nines.

Boys usually wear a miniversion of the groomsmen's tuxedo, or the closest thing available in their size (possibly with a clip-on version of the tie for easy dressing on the big day).

For flower girls, there are more options. Most flower-girl dresses are white or ivory and floor-length, and they can be as simple or as intricate as you like. The flower girl may also wear a similar dress to that of the bridesmaids, or a dress with a white top and a skirt in one of the wedding colors.

TOP: *Appropriately clad, a proud mother-of-the-bride poses with her daughter and the maid of honor.* BOTTOM: *A flower girl in her cloche hat and coat lingers in the church after the wedding ceremony has ended.* RIGHT: *A nervous ring bearer rehearses the motions in his head.*

7 SMART SHOPPING
making the most of your outings to the store

Of April, May, of June, and July flowers.
I sing of maypoles, hock-harts, wassails, wakes,
Of Bridegrooms, Brides, and of their bridal cakes.

—*Robert Herrick,* Hesperides *(1648)*

Okay, you've found "the one." Now it's time to begin another search—the search for "the one" wedding dress that makes your heart melt almost as much as your special guy. And just like you "knew" when you found the love of your life, you'll know when you've found the right dress—there will be no question in your mind.

To find that special dress, you've got to be a smart, savvy shopper. In short, you have to be prepared. Map out your budget and plan of attack before you even think of setting foot in a bridal salon. Without a plan, you'll be vulnerable to the two biggest wedding dress–shopping mistakes: overspending and hasty decision making. Here's how to get ready.

BEFORE YOU START SHOPPING

First of all, leave yourself plenty of time. The last thing you want to do is buy a wedding dress in panic mode, so make sure you allow plenty of shopping days before the wedding. It takes four to six months for some dresses to come in, so leave at least that much time before the big day. Don't forget the time for fittings and alterations if necessary. From there, follow these pre-shopping pieces of advice:

RIGHT: *Your wedding gown should match the surroundings. The more formal the reception hall, the more formal the gown should be.*

OPPOSITE: *This elegant strapless floor-length gown is perfect for the bridesmaid with an hourglass figure.*

Create your backdrop

Your wedding dress should match the surroundings in which it will be seen—during both the ceremony and the reception. If you're getting married in a flower garden, you'll go for something a little more flowing and romantic; if you're tying the knot in a candle-lit church, you may want a more formal look. And because it's easier (believe it or not!) to find a gown than a church, temple, or reception hall, it's best to book those places first, and then start looking for an appropriate dress for your venues.

Know your budget

A price point will limit a seemingly overwhelming selection of to-die-for gowns in a hurry. To save yourself time and heartache, calculate what you can spend before you start shopping. If you know you absolutely have to stay under $1,000 you won't even be tempted to try on that $20,000 Vera Wang (okay, you may be tempted, but you'll be less likely to allow yourself to carry it into the dressing room).

Peruse magazines

Do a little pre-shopping research at your local magazine stand. Page through the latest bridal magazines and look for women who are similar in size, shape, and likeness to you. Once you've found your look-alikes, tear out the pictures and create a small scrapbook of styles you love. Then carry your scrapbook with you as you shop so you can emulate the looks.

Do your homework

When choosing the stores or bridal salons you want to visit, don't cast too wide or too narrow a net. Before you pick your stores, review the websites of some popular shops in your area for their philosophy, available sizes, price ranges, and services. If you want to be pampered and you don't mind shelling out a few extra bucks, full-service bridal salons are your best bet. If you'd rather wade through racks of gowns on your own and pay a little less, you'll be better off at a discount outlet. Ideally, you'll want to narrow down your list of shops to about four and then conduct a phone interview with each.

Interrogate

During your bridal salon phone interviews, pay attention to the way you're treated—if the staff are friendly and eager to help over the phone, they'll probably have the same behavior in person. Consider asking the following questions, along with any others you think of:

- How much do wedding dresses at your store cost (range)?

- Which designers do you carry?

- What sizes do you carry?

- Do you do fittings and alterations at your store, or are they done at a different location?

- Are the fittings included in the price? If not, how much extra do they cost?

- Do you sell accessories, such as veils, headpieces, shoes, and other items?

- Do you offer any package deals with accessories or bridesmaids' dresses?

- Do you offer any guarantees on your wedding dresses? If so, what are they?

After the phone interviews, narrow your search further to two or three stores—any more than that is probably too many.

Mark your calendar

Plan to spend about one to three hours in each shop and mark your calendar accordingly. If you're a marathon shopper, you may be able to do more than one shop in a day. If you tend to get frustrated and cranky easily, limit yourself to one store a day.

Consider sample sales

If you're a budget-minded person who still values high quality, you may want to hit a few sample sales—they offer wedding dresses that have been tried on by customers and may have some minor blemishes, such as makeup stains. You'll make out particularly well at a sample sale if you're a size 6, 8, or 10 (three of the most popular sizes).

Think about shopping online

If you're not a shop-til-you-drop type and you prefer to do most of your shopping via your home computer, consider looking for a wedding gown online. Some brides have had tremendous success with sites such as eBay. One bride found an $1,800 Demetrios gown she had earlier ruled out on eBay and got it for a steal—$402!

the wedding gown book

ONE WOMAN'S STORY

I borrowed my first wedding gown, in 1962, from my girlfriend's cousin. She happened to be the same size as me. My parents and I didn't have enough money to make a wedding to begin with, so when she offered me the dress, I said yes. In fact, I don't even remember going to look for a gown. I do remember, however, going to look at tiaras and head-pieces and buying one for myself. I also remember that my mother-in-law bought me a beautiful beaded pocketbook for my wedding day, and I kept it for many years.

For my second wedding, in 1983, I wore a champagne-colored dress, as I didn't think it was appropriate to wear white. Because the wedding was a brunch, I wore a mid-calf-length dress and a hat, rather than a veil.

The real difference between my first wedding dress and my second wedding dress, however, was my attitude. Even though I still didn't have that much money to spare, I told myself that I would buy the dress I wanted to wear no matter what the cost. I loved my second dress, loved how I looked, and was just so very happy. In fact, my second husband and I got married a second time in a church, because the first wedding was a civil union. That was four years later, and because I had gained about five pounds, I couldn't breathe.

–Bev Pagano, New Jersey

HAVING YOUR DRESS MADE

Before heading out to the stores, you might also consider having your gown made for you. There are a number of reasons that this plan may work better for you. First, you may have a very specific idea of what you want and aren't seeing that idea on the racks of gowns that fill the stores. Or perhaps you are difficult to fit and would rather spend money on a custom gown than vastly alter a gown that isn't quite what you wanted in the first place.

If you want to have your dress made for you the first thing you must consider is time. Most wedding gown seamstresses are booked far in advance, so give yourself and her at least a year to work on the dress.

If you don't know a seamstress, go to a fabric store. They usually have a list of women who specialize in wedding gowns. And, while you're at the fabric store, take a look at their pattern books, as well as the fabrics on display. The large fabric stores usually devote a section of the store to wedding gowns, so you'll be able to see the differences between ivory satin and natural silk shantung, as well as a variety of laces.

Feel free to bring pictures from magazines of what you would like and be specific about what aspects of the gown you like and what you think won't work for you. For example, you might like the beading on one gown and the neckline on another. Ask the seamstress whether she can combine the looks or details of two or more gowns in a way that will work. Not all dress details are complementary.

With that in mind, make sure you listen to the seamstress's opinion. Remember, her experience working with fabric and understanding which designs flatter specific body types is invaluable. She should know what a dress needs to hold its shape, lay properly, and look appropriate for your size and shape, and the time and style of your wedding.

HITTING THE SHOPS

The homework's done, so put on your shopping shoes and get ready to go! Here are some tips to help you conquer the shops and salons.

Choose your shopping partner or partners wisely

This is not a time for your "yes" friend or your most critical pal. You want someone who will be patient, positive, open-minded, and (politely) honest with you about what looks great and what doesn't. And of course, you want her (or him) to have good taste!

LEFT: *For the most pleasant shopping experience, take your most patient, supportive, understanding friends who will help you choose wisely— and make sure you have fun while doing so.*

BELOW: *Do not forget to "think wearability" while shopping. Can you sit comfortably in your gown? Does the dress drape gracefully as you move?*

Pack a bag of accessories	To get the truest sense of what a dress will look like on the big day, try it on with some extras, such as shoes, a strapless or backless bra, a slip, and some jewelry. You don't have to buy the accessories before you get the dress—just grab some things from home that are similar to items you will ultimately want to pair with your dress, such as pearls and dressy shoes.
Realize that wedding gowns are the opposite of vanity-sized	In contrast to jeans, which tend to be oversized to make shoppers feel good about their size (so a woman who is a size 14 strolls out of the store gleefully with a size 10), wedding gowns usually run smaller than your typical size. If you typically wear a size 8, for example, you'll probably wear a 10 or 12 in a wedding gown. So be ready to let the ego go!
Be adventurous	Ironically, you don't necessarily have to stay married to your typical clothing style when it comes to your wedding gown. If you're a conservative dresser, go out on a fashion limb and try on some more dramatic, riskier styles. Or if you're usually attention-getting with your clothes, try on a few classic, understated gowns. Just as with love, sometimes opposites attract in a wedding gown relationship.
Think wearability	You want your wedding dress to look amazing, but not at the price of comfort. You'll have to wear the dress for close to 12 hours, and you'll be sitting, standing, dancing, and hugging. So when you try on the dress, practice all the moves you foresee yourself making in it and check for any riding, pinching, or bunching. If it doesn't feel as good as it looks, forget it and keep looking.
Don't overestimate weight loss	Many brides have a weight goal in mind for their wedding day, but to be frank, many fail to achieve it. To avoid a wedding day zipper war, buy your dress for the size you are, not the size you want to be. You can always take it in if you lose weight.
If you are buying a designer dress, make sure it's legit	It may seem cruel to dupe a giddy bride into buying a fake designer gown for a real designer price, but it happens. To make sure it doesn't happen to you, research stores before you shop them. The rule: For an upscale dress, go to an upscale boutique.
Play model	If the salon permits photographs, bring a camera along with you and ask your shopping partner to snap some shots of you in your favorite gowns. You'll be able to review your options at home and ask friends and family members which dress is most stunning on you.

Take notes	After a full day of shopping, all the images of lace and silk, ivory and champagne may start to blur, so keep track of the dresses you've tried on by taking notes. For each gown, write down exactly what you liked and disliked.
Don't go by a photo alone	A picture says a thousand words … except when it comes to wedding gowns. Fabric textures and colors can look vastly different in person than they do in a catalog, so don't commit to a special order without seeing at least a swatch of the fabric and color you've chosen.
Be prepared to make a down payment	Once you find the gem, be prepared to make a 50 to 60 percent deposit on it, preferably on a credit card for added insurance. And keep in mind that in most cases, this deposit cannot be canceled or refunded. Once you order it, the gown is yours. So before you put any money down, ask when the final payment is due and what it includes.
Get it in writing	Just in case something goes awry (you may think it won't happen to you, but many brides have wedding dress horror stories to tell), it's wise to write the date of delivery, size, manufacturer, and gown details directly on your sales receipt. That way, you have proof of what you were promised and when.
Inquire about alteration and fitting fees	Alterations typically cost about $100, depending on the sleeves, lining, and detail, but they can run all the way up to $300. Get an estimate of how many fittings will be required and how much each will cost up front, so you're not stuck with a big shock at the end.
Don't feel compelled to spend thousands	In these economically challenged times, most brides have more important things to spend big bucks on than a wedding gown, so they're not dropping a pretty penny. Luckily, to please fashion-conscious but frugal brides, the bridal industry is making beautiful gowns for not that much money. Many bridal salons sell gowns for as little as $99, and they're still gorgeous.

OPPOSITE RIGHT:
It's wise to narrow your choices down to a select few before you decide on "the one."
OPPOSITE FAR RIGHT: *Your perfect, flawless gown may be another woman's least favorite: be sure to keep an open mind.*

8 ALTERNATIVE GOWNS
options for brides who don't want the long white dress

Love, be true to her; Life, be dear to her;
Health, stay close to her; Joy, draw near to her;
Fortune, find what you can do for her;
Search your treasure-house through
and through for her,
Follow her footsteps the wide world over—
And keep her husband always her lover.

—Anna Lewis, "To the Bride"

ABOVE: *If you're not sold on a traditional shade of white for your dress, embrace an array of colors. Truly, on your day, anything goes.* OPPOSITE: *This stunning blue strapless is an excellent choice for a bridesmaid... or the bride.*

You've dreamt about the romance, the proposal, the first dance, and maybe even the cake. But in your fantasies, for whatever reasons, the dress isn't traditional, poofy, or princess-esque. Maybe you can't afford a wedding gown. Or perhaps you're getting married on an exotic tropical island, you're getting ready to say "I do" for the second time, or you're pregnant. Whatever your situation may be, the perfect dress is out there. It's just a matter of finding it.

First, recognize your options for places to purchase your gown. Because you're not locked into any particular style, the sky is pretty much the limit. Here are some ideas to help you.

Browse bridal salons	Many bridal salons offer nontraditional gown options in terms of styles and colors, including soft pinks and blues, metallic shades of copper and silver, or even deeper shades such as magenta, black, and red. Or you may fall in love with a bridesmaid's gown that you can substitute for a wedding gown.

Check out department stores	Consider perusing the women's section of your local department store. You may find an evening gown, a holiday gown, a cocktail dress, or even a prom ensemble that's perfect for you. Right after the holidays is a great time to shop for an evening gown, because they're marked way down. For a prom dress, the ideal time to shop is in March or April. Many prom dresses are very tasteful and stylish, and they come in a range of sizes (so if you're intimidated by wearing a dress made for a teenager, don't be). If you end up purchasing a dress from a department store, just make sure you choose something that's somewhat obscure—you don't want to wear the same dress as one of your guests.
Rent a gown	If you don't mind literally filling other brides' shoes, and you're not planning to do the sentimental "saving the gown" thing, consider renting a wedding gown. The process is similar to renting men's formalwear—the alterations and cleaning are usually included in the price.
Go for a theme	To stand out from the weddings of their friends, many brides are opting for a theme wedding. Angel themes are quite popular, with wedding gowns decorated with feathers and wings for the bridesmaids and/or flower girls. Or you can go for a movie theme, such as a Disney wedding, where you, your husband to be, and your attendants all become characters from a particular movie, such as Beauty and the Beast, Cinderella, or even The Little Mermaid. You can rent these costumes at a costume shop for a fraction of the price of buying a gown, and most reputable shops will do the alterations for you. Or you can also highlight the place you and your husband met in a theme wedding. If you met in college, for example, feature your school colors somewhere in your ensemble.
Celebrate your heritage	As if they weren't happy enough, your parents will be extra proud if you feature your family's heritage in your look. For instance, a bride with Japanese ancestors might wear a kimono, a bride from Morocco might wear the traditional caftan, or a Scottish bride might wear a tasteful plaid throw over her gown.

RIGHT: *A corset style strapless gown incorporates classic black detailing into its embellishments.*

Borrow your gown

There's something extra sweet and sentimental about a bride wearing her mother or grandmother's wedding dress. Of course, you should never feel obligated to wear a dress that you don't absolutely love, but if your mother's dress is your style or your grand-mother's dress is back in vogue, go for it. Keep in mind that you'll probably have to make some fairly significant alterations on a borrowed dress, especially if the first person that wore it was a lot larger or smaller than you.

Run away

In these footloose and fancy-free times, destination weddings are becoming increasingly popular. Instead of the typical church and reception hall, many brides are exchanging their vows somewhere a little different, such as on a sun-kissed beach, in a hot air balloon, at a Vegas chapel, or on a cobblestone lane in Italy. If you're getting married out of town, your dress should match your venue…and be easy to pack.

Many destination brides go with a gown that's light, flowing, and carefree (depending on the weather where they're tying the knot, of course). And some beach brides wear nothing but a bikini top and sarong. But if your destination is a faraway formal chapel, you can still go with a traditional gown with a 20-foot (6.1 m) train—it's entirely up to you.

One idea for a destination wedding is to incorporate some of the elements of your surroundings into your gown. If you're getting hitched on a tropical island, put some of the native flowers in your hair, around your neck, or around your wrist. You can even attach flowers to your gown along the neck or backline.

Transform your dress

For two looks in one, cover an elegant, simple white party dress with an intricate overlay, such as a lace jacket that runs the entire length of the skirt. Wear the jacket for the ceremony and then whip it off for the reception!

ABOVE: *Illusion fabric allows skin to show through without baring all.*
OPPOSITE: *For two looks in one, pair your gown with a pretty jacket, like this tulle overlay.*

LEFT: *A simple sheath dress can be made more feminine with a flowing tulle veil and a Chantilly lace slip that protrudes an inch or two below the hem.*

Have a gown custom made

This is not an option for the budget-conscious bride, but having a custom-made dress will allow you to create exactly what you want for yourself, from head to toe. Many brides are taking elements they love from a variety of dresses and showing them to their designers. For example, they'll look through a bridal magazine and ask a designer to create a dress that features the neckline of one dress, the sleeves of a second dress, and the skirt of a third. Most designers welcome the opportunity to do this because it gives them ideas for future designs. One note of caution, however: If you're having your dress made, allow plenty of time for your dress to be completed before the big day.

Decorate your dress

If you're strapped for cash or just have the urge to be creative, find a simple white slip dress and decorate it with pearls, beads, or crystals. If you're handy with a needle and thread, you can do this yourself, or you can pick out the embellishments and have them attached professionally.

Go extra simple

If you're not a lace and frills type of bride, go for a simple white sundress or party dress. You certainly won't have problems finding one, and you'll probably save a bundle. And if you want guests to notice your face more than your gown, place the pizzazz on your head, with an elegant headpiece or feminine flowers.

ONE WOMAN'S STORY

In April 1999 I was finally able to summon up the courage to call the man of my dreams and ask him "out" on a date. (I had been pining away for him for at least a year...maybe longer.) When he agreed to come to my house for a game of Scrabble, I believed I was in heaven.

Fast forward one month: I am in Washington, DC with my sister Mary, and my daughter, Rochelle. We spend a humid day shopping in Alexandria, Virginia—mostly at eclectic shops. In one vintage clothing store, I spotted a dress that screamed late-1960s. It had to be mine because I knew it would someday be a wedding dress. No one else on earth could wear that dress and get away with it.

It is a long, quilted cotton/polyester dress, with three-quarter-length sleeves, and an invisible zipper (remember those?) The print is of giant paisleys with pinks, oranges, and just a hint of lime green.

And yes, I did wear it to our backyard wedding on June 28, 2003—along with white sneakers and Gumby earrings.

—Odette Gornick, Maine

unveiled
NONTRADITIONAL SITUATIONS

These days, not every bride is a virgin getting married for the first time. Many brides are on their second wedding, have children from previous relationships, or are pregnant when they say "I do."

for the second-time-around bride

Because first-run brides are bending the rules so much, you don't necessarily have to do anything radically different. There's not so much distinction between first-time brides and those who are getting married for a second, third, or fourth time. Most brides getting married for the second (or more) time go a little less for the bridal and a little more for the style. But if you want the traditional long white dress, that's fine, too. You can consider incorporating your or your groom's children into the ceremony as well, from serving as the ring bearer, flower girl, usher, or bridesmaid.

for the pregnant bride

If you're expecting, you'll be glowing extra brightly on your wedding day. Don't try to hide your pregnancy—celebrate it! Don't be afraid to show off your full form with a plunging neckline or a waist that accentuates your belly. Having said that, you don't want to go with something that has a tight fit, because you'll probably be bigger than you anticipated when the day rolls around. A good cut for a pregnant bride is the empire, where the waist comes out from underneath the bustline. And make sure you wear comfortable shoes that provide extra support.

If you really want to show off your baby on board, check out the stretchy, sexy, form-fitting lace wedding gowns by Nicole Michelle at www.nicolematernity.com and have a ball.

ABOVE: *These days, there's not much distinction between the attire for a bride who's getting married for the first time and a bride who's tying the knot for a second... or third...time around.*

107

ALTERNATIVE GOWNS

"Keep your eyes wide open before marriage, half shut afterwards."

—*Benjamin Franklin*

Historically, the first wedding veils were symbols of submissiveness and a bride's promise to obey her new husband; only after the ceremony could the veil be lifted, revealing the bride's appearance to the groom for the first time.

Though this tradition may seem dated, there is still something very cool about the "unveiling" of a glowing bride on her wedding day—especially because today the groom knows and loves his bride's face. And headpieces— once used solely to secure the veil—can now be a very important, fun part of the bridal ensemble.

But veils and headpieces are not a must. In these "anything goes" times, you can choose to adorn your head and face as much or as little as you like. If you do opt for some head decorations, stay in the same color tones as your dress. Whether it's hair jewelry, a tiara, or a veil, the colors should complement your gown. For instance, if your dress is a crisp white, look for a headpiece with white pearls, rhinestones, Australian crystals, or baby blue crystals. If your dress is a warmer tone, go for ivory pearls, ivory crystals, or embellishments in gold or topaz shades.

A LESSON IN VEILS AND VEIL STYLES

Just like wedding dresses, veils are now available in more styles, lengths, and fabrics than ever before. Rhinestone edging, gilded thread embroidery, and custom-made lengths are regular buzzwords in the veil industry.

Usually made from a soft silk or a nylon netting fabric called tulle or illusion (think of a ballet tutu), veils come in gold, silver, and blush tones, as well as the standard white, diamond, and ivory.

TOP: *You can wear your veil over your face for a more dramatic, time-honored look.*
BOTTOM: *Spanish in origin, mantilla veils consist of a drape of lace worn without a headpiece. They may be short or long.*
OPPOSITE: *A windswept ballet veil temporarily takes center stage.*

ABOVE: *The angel veil is perfect for the minimalist bride who wants an element of tradition.*

Traditionally, brides wear a longer veil during the ceremony and a shorter one at the reception, but as with most areas of wedding attire, veil traditions are often ignored. Because of cost and convenience, many modern brides are getting one short veil for the entire event.

Depending on how you're styling your hair, you can pin your veil at the bottom of your head below your bun (to make a more subdued statement) or you can attach it more prominently to your headpiece.

To create an extra-special look with your veil, consider adornments such as Alençon lace appliqué, rhinestone trimming, delicate beading, all-over crystals, or patterns of gilded threads.

Angel		This is a simple, ungathered, square-cut veil that creates a minimalist look.
Ballet (waltz)		Best with an ankle-length dress, the ballet veil falls to the bride's ankles.
Blusher		This is a loose veil that's worn back over the head-piece or forward over the face and then attaches to a longer, two- or three-tiered veil. Blusher veils go best with a shorter dress.
Cathedral		Usually worn with a long, cathedral train, a cathedral veil flows about 3½ yards (3.2 m) from the headpiece.
Chapel		Slightly shorter than the cathedral veil, a chapel veil is a long, cascading veil that falls about 2⅓ yards (2.1 m) from the headpiece. Chapel and cathedral veils go best with dresses with a train.
Circular		This is a simple, ungathered, flowing veil that attaches to the head with combs.

ABOVE: *The most popular veil length, the fingertip veil is a compromise between fun and formal.*

Fingertip

The most popular veil length, a fingertip veil falls across the shoulders and down to the fingertips when the arms are extended.

Flyaway or waterfall

A more casual veil with multiple layers that brush the shoulders, this style is an ideal match for a dress with an exquisite back.

Mantilla

This is a drape of lace worn without a headpiece. Spanish in origin, mantilla veils may be short or long.

Poof

This is a short veil that rises from the headpiece and cascades down the back.

A LESSON IN HEADPIECES

When selecting a headpiece to top off your look, keep your personal style, intended hairdo, and face shape in mind. If your face is long and narrow, for example, you'll look best in a headpiece that widens your face, such as a picture hat or a floral wreath. If your face is round and full, add height with a pillbox hat or a tiara. Here are some of your options.

Coronet		Usually adorned with satin and lace, a coronet is a crescent-shaped headpiece that rests high on the crown of the head.
Hair jewelry		In lieu of a larger headpiece, you can choose to accessorize your hair with jeweled, beaded, or laced hair combs, clips, or sticks.
Headband		A simple, elegant look, headbands extend over the top of the head from temple to temple.
Juliet cap		This is a cap that fits snugly on the crown of the head and is ornately decorated with pearls, sequins, or beads.
Picture hat		A picture hat is a dramatic hat with a very large brim, often decorated with elaborate patterns of lace, beads, jewels, or sequins.
Pillbox hat		This is a small, brimless hat shaped like a pillbox (still widely associated with Jackie Kennedy).
Profile		A large, decorative comb, a profile can be worn on the side or back of the head.
Snood		If you're wearing your hair in a bun, you can cover the bun in a small, woven piece of fabric called a snood.

TOP: *Simple and pretty, a head-band gives the allure of innocence.*
BOTTOM: *An elegant alternative to a hair piece is an updo decorated with tiny ornate pins.*
OPPOSITE: *This coronet is ornately decorated with tiny beads.*

Tiara

The classic Cinderella-style tiara will never go out of style, so you can't go wrong with one. Tiaras are worn high on the head (not at the hairline—a mistake many brides make); they range from simple to lavish, and are usually encrusted with crystals, pearls, or lace. With a half-up, half-down hairstyle, tiaras create a pretty princess look. But keep in mind that tiaras can be one of the most expensive pieces of a wedding ensemble—many cost $500 or more. So if you'd rather not have to take out a loan for your tiara, consider another headpiece option, such as a starter—a miniature tiara, about 5 inches (13 cm) across, that attaches to the head with combs.

Wreath

Wreaths encircle your entire head or bun and can be decorated with whatever you choose, from diamonds to lace to flowers. Floral wreaths are a beautiful and inexpensive option. You can make a floral wreath yourself, or ask your florist to put one together to complement your colors.

TOP: *Tiaras can also be simple and understated, drawing more attention to the bride's face.*
BOTTOM: *A bride can't go wrong with the classic Cinderella-inspired tiara.*

ONE WOMAN'S STORY

I went to Kleinfeld's to look at dresses and was assigned a very motherly saleslady who did not approve of my desire to wear a very simple sheath dress for my June wedding. She allowed me to try on half a dozen or so dresses, but after about an hour, she stormed out of the dressing room to "see what else she could find." She returned with a stunning, custom-made gown that had been ordered but never picked up by the bride (I'm sure that bride has a good story!). I suppose they were just storing it in a back room or something until they figured out what to do with it.

It was silk shantung with a full skirt and dozens of handmade silk flowers with pearl stamens along the neckline. It had a beautiful bustle in the back and fit me like a glove. When I turned to show the saleslady the dress, she exclaimed, "Now, that's how a bride should look!"

I had looked at enough dresses to know what heavy silk shantung cost, not to mention the hours and hours of handwork that went into creating that dress. I looked at the tag, and it said $7,000. The saleslady saw me looking and hurried over. She put her arm around me and said, "Honey, that's the price for the original bride. Because we have to sell it as a sample, you'll get it for $1,000." I felt like she was some kind of wedding gown fairy godmother or something because not only did she find me the perfect dress (which was unlike anything I had been drawn to previously) but she gave it to me at the perfect price as well.

–Holly Schmidt, Massachusetts

unveiled

HAIRSTYLES

Your hairstyle on your wedding day should be personalized to your style, wedding dress, veil, and headpiece. It can be anything froma low knot at the base of your neck to curls at the top of your head.

Formal, updo styles are most popular, but free-flowing natural styles are perfectly acceptable as well. Whichever style you choose, keep these tips in mind.

Research your style

When it comes to hairstyles, a picture is worth a thousand words. If you find a look you love in a magazine, take the picture to your stylist and ask him or her to recreate it for you.

TOP: *Very short hair can be stunning on a bride, accentuating fine bone structure and complementing the entire look.* BOTTOM: *A half up, half down hair style coupled with colorful, bold flowers can create drama.*

Stand out in a crowd

You're the bride, and you should be the center of attention, apart from your brides-maids. So style your hair differently from the bridesmaids—if they're wearing their hair up, wear yours down and coiffed out. If they're wearing their hair down, wear yours up in a formal style.

Wash your hair the night before

If you're wearing your hair up, refrain from washing it the morning of the big day. Slightly dirty hair styles better and produces fewer flyaways.

Wear an easy-access shirt

The last thing you want to do is ruin your perfectly styled head by pulling a T-shirt over it, so wear a shirt with buttons in the front to your hair appointment so you can change your clothes with ease.

Go for a trial run

To avoid getting a "bride of Frankenstein" shock of your life on the big day, ask your stylist to go through a trial run on your hair a week or so before. This will probably cost you, but it will be well worth it!

CHARLOTTE: *"I just feel kind of silly that I made such a big fuss about my ring earlier."*

SAMANTHA: *"Oh, honey, a diamond that big deserves a parade!"*

—Kristin Davis to Kim Catrall on Sex and the City

ABOVE: *Pearls and lace— the perfect wedding accessories.*
OPPOSITE: *Every flower has a special meaning and can convey a particular message.*

Once upon a time, a bride adorned herself with every piece of jewelry she owned on her wedding day. Today, brides are more concerned with showing themselves off than showing off their jewels, and understated is the most popular rule of thumb.

At this point, you've spent a lot of time, effort, and money choosing your special dress, a dress that's absolutely perfect for you in every way. So naturally, you want your accessories to complement—not distract from—the dress you've worked so hard to find.

Accessorizing your dress should be the very last thing you do, after you've ordered your veil and headpiece. As you accessorize, keep your dress in mind at all times (as if you could forget it), and choose modest pieces that won't steal the show. As a general rule, the more sparkles on your dress, the fewer you should add with your accessories. And if you choose a flashier necklace, go with minimalist earrings and vice versa.

Also, make sure your accessories are in concert with the overall feel and formality of the wedding. Use your best judgment here. Don't wear rhinestones to an afternoon outdoor ceremony or strappy sandals without hose for a dimly lit, evening wedding. If you're having trouble making accessory decisions, go with your gut instinct. You can never go wrong when you stick with your personal style.

JAZZ YOURSELF UP WITH JEWELRY

When done right, jewelry can add special sparkle and life to your wedding day appearance.

The veil and headpiece are a central part of your look, so start with those pieces and then select jewelry to match, moving downward to earrings, then a necklace, then bracelets, and so forth.

Whatever jewelry you choose, don't date yourself with a style that's too trendy. Instead, stick with the tried and true—diamonds, pearls, and classic, timeless looks that will look wonderful in your photographs 20 years down the road.

picking pearls

In most cases, you can't go wrong with a simple strand of pearls matched with tasteful drop or stud pearl earrings. When selecting pearls, first decide what you want to spend and get a sense of the style you're going for. Pearls come in two basic lengths: choker (14" to 16" [36 cm to 41 cm]) and princess (17" to 19" [43 cm to 48 cm]). If strands aren't your thing but you still love pearls, consider a simple chain with a drop pearl.

Pearls come in a range of white shades and colors, from ivory to black to peach, and it's important to match the right shade with your dress. If your dress is a crisp white, choose stark-white pearls as opposed to creamier ones. For a more dramatic look, consider black (Tahitian) pearls, which stand out beautifully next to white silks and satins.

If your dress is an off-white shade of ivory or champagne, try to match your pearls as closely as you can to the exact color of the dress. For a soft pink, peach, or platinum dress, go for a strand of white, ivory, or silvery pearls. To make sure you get it right, carry a swatch of your fabric when shopping for your pearls.

If the price of a strand of cultured pearls sends you into a state of shock, look into freshwater pearls. They're very pretty, and an entire necklace usually goes for less than $100.00.

ABOVE: *Pearls should match the shade of the gown. For an ivory dress, go with ivory pearls; for a stark white dress, go with white pearls.*
OPPOSITE: *Classic, timeless jewelry pieces will look wonderful in your photographs 20 years down the road.*

BELOW: *Classic and refined, drop pearls will never go out of style.*

RIGHT: *Sophisticated and bold, chandelier earrings can be gorgeous, especially when your hair is pulled back.*

OPPOSITE: *Drop or chandelier earrings look wonderful with a low cut dress.*

WHY THE GARTER AND BOUQUET TOSS?

For the origin of the garter and bridal bouquet toss we have to go back quite a ways. It was customary in the fourteenth century for the bride to toss her garter to the men. Sometimes the men would get drunk, become impatient, and try to remove the garter ahead of time. Therefore, the custom evolved for the groom to remove and toss the garter. And with that change, the bride started tossing the bridal bouquet to the unwed women of marriageable age. After all, why should the guys have all the fun?

decorate yourself

If your dress has a simple bodice, a single diamond solitaire pendant or a delicate sterling silver or white-gold necklace will be classic and beautiful.

If your dress is decorated with crystals, consider going with a bare neck or a simple silver chain adorned with crystals to match your dress.

For your ears, diamond solitaire earrings will flatter just about any dress. For a dress on the simpler side, ornate antique-style chandelier earrings will be a beautiful complement. And diamond or pearl drop earrings look wonderful with a lower cut dress, especially if you plan to wear your hair up.

Bracelets are tricky with a wedding dress. You'll be carrying a bouquet, so you don't want too much going on with your arms. If your sleeves are capped or short, or if your gown is sleeveless, you can wear a pearl, diamond, silver, or gold bracelet. Forego a bracelet if your sleeves are long.

ʃunveiled
THE SECRET LANGUAGE OF JEWELRY

He asked you to marry him and, we presume, slipped onto your finger a beautiful ring, most likely a diamond, but perhaps an amethyst or an emerald. Jewelry is, in many ways, as important as your gown to the look and symbolism of your wedding. Many women choose family pearls to wear with their wedding gown, but according to gemologists, mythologists, and spiritual advisers, each gemstone has its own magical meaning. Knowing the significance of each stone, as well as the ways specific pieces of jewelry can protect you, may help you choose the jewelry you wear on your wedding day.

Necklaces, pendants, and chokers

A necklace or choker opens the throat chakra, or energy center ruling communication and music (the voice). A strand of pearls not only looks timelessly elegant but also boosts your self-esteem and sociability (because you can speak freely and with animation). The best metals for necklaces on your special day are silver, copper, and gold.

Earrings

Earrings were once worn to guard the ears from potential disease and from hearing bad news. They were also believed to strengthen weak eyes, especially if set with emeralds. Earrings help balance both hemispheres of the brain and can also stabilize the throat chakra. The earlobes are sensory centers on the body and usually benefit from the stimulation of a gem or crystal. Jade and tigereye are great for reviving and refreshing. Sapphires will bring you greater wisdom. Lapis lazuli and opal, however, can be overstimulating, so watch carefully and see how your body reacts to them. Some people feel lightheaded with these two stones placed so high on the body. Malachite can be too spiritually stimulating for earrings; don't wear it unless you want to be in a soulful or dreamy reverie. Pearl earrings calm and clear the mind. Garnet earrings will enhance your popularity. And here is a tip that might soon cause a stampede to the jewelry shop: Rose quartz is wonderful for the skin and can even slow aging! It's also a symbol for love—perfect for your wedding day.

ABOVE: *A bride and groom's wedding bands can match... or they can be distinctly different.*
LEFT: *This simple dress can afford dramatic, bold jewelry, such as this collection of pearl chokers.*

Chains	Chains represent links between people, the ties that bind you to another. Other mystical associations for chains are happiness and justice; prayer; reason and the soul; communication and command. Plato referred to a golden chain linking the earth to the heavens above, a bond between humans and immortals. Socrates tied our human happiness to the concept of justice with a chain of steel and diamonds. You can wear chains as jewelry or as part of the pattern in your wedding gown.
Rings	Rings represent eternity, unity, reincarnation, safety, union, power, and energy. They symbolize the eternity of the circle shape—the universe. Wearing rings was believed to help ward off any kind of malevolence; through their continuity, nothing could get in. A ring binds you with the energy of the stone. In dream psychology, a ring represents the desire for reconciliation of the different parts of your being and personality; it shows you want to be an integrated whole, which is the first step in making it happen. If you want to deepen your friendship with your spouse, exchange amber rings to bind you together forever. Native Americans wear turquoise rings because it is a guardian stone; its power is doubled when it is in a ring. The ring finger is about creativity, and, of course, the ring finger on the left hand is your love center and a direct connection to your heart. For deep and loyal ties of love, wear a diamond. To express your love, wear a moonstone.
Brooches	Brooches were the costume jewelry of the medieval Irish, who decorated themselves with gems and valuable stones to show they were part of the aspiring warrior caste. Brooches symbolize virginity, faithfulness, and protection. A diamond-studded brooch is a double symbol of love and safeguarding.
Bracelets	The wrists are perfect pulse points. Organic gems, such as coral and abalone, are very helpful for energy flow and release. Turquoise is great for stabilizing and calming you physically.
Ankle bracelets and toe rings	Bejeweled feet and ankles are very sexy. Jewelry in this area of the body is also grounding and stabilizing. If you are dealing with anxiety or substance-abuse issues, wear amethyst around your ankle. If you're feeling drained of energy, jasper or rock crystal will come in handy. Rhodonite will do the trick if you are feeling disconnected or restless.

TOP: *Like Cinderella's shoes, the bride's shoes should be a perfect fit, so she can walk, stand, and dance with ease.*
BOTTOM: *Pretty shoes are the finishing touch to a pretty bride.*

STEP OUT IN STYLISH SHOES

With all the focus on your gown, you may be tempted to cut back on your wedding-day footwear. Bad idea. You will be on your feet dancing, hugging, and posing for photographs for at least eight hours, and nothing will ruin an enchanted day faster than a set of sore feet. Choose your shoes wisely.

You certainly don't want cheap, clunky shoes to peek out from your princess-like charmeuse skirt; but you don't want to be secretly wincing all day because your feet are killing you either. The combination of style and comfort in a pair of shoes is as desirable a blend as looks and intelligence in a man. It's possible to find both in footwear, you just may have to spend a little more money.

The single most important tip for wedding-day shoes is this: Have two pairs—one pretty pair for the ceremony, such as a classic silk heel with beading or embroidery, and a second, more practical and comfortable pair, such as a platform wedgy shoe or a sneaker style, for the reception. Make sure the comfy pair of shoes is close to the same heel height as the first pair (otherwise your dress will drag on the ground once you make the switch). Here are some additional tips:

WHY SHOES ON THE BACK OF YOUR GET-AWAY CAR?
The tradition of tying shoes to the back of the couple's car stems from Tudor times. Back then, guests would throw shoes at the bride and groom. If they or their carriage were hit, it meant good luck would be bestowed upon them. In Anglo-Saxon times, the groom, to establish his authority, symbolically struck the bride with a shoe. Brides would then throw a shoe at the bridesmaids to see who would marry next. Makes you appreciate the bouquet toss, doesn't it?

Know your options	There's much more available in wedding footwear than your standard white pump. If you're a real shoe buff, you're in luck. There are a ton of gorgeous, glamorous shoes out there adorned with crystals, pearls, jewels, bows, silk flowers, or ribbons. And metallic gold or silver shoes can be a classy, stylish alternative to traditional white or dyeable shoes.

Here's what you have to choose from in terms of shoe style:

- **Dyed shoes:** Shoes that can be dyed to match the color of your fabric, whether it's white, ivory, or pink.
- **Classic pump:** A formal shoe that's closed at the toe and heel.
- **Sling-back pump:** Pump with a closed toe and open heel with a strap across the back.
- **Open-toed pump:** Pump with an open toe and closed back. Note: If you're going to wear any style of open-toed shoe, don't wear hose—hose with open toes are a major fashion faux pas!
- **Sandal:** A high-heeled shoe with an open toe and heel. (Remember: no hose!)
- **Mule:** A closed-toed shoe with an open heel.
- **Flat:** A comfortable, low-heeled shoe that's best with a long, full skirt.
- **Slipper:** A flat, soft shoe with minimal support that's best with a long, full skirt.
- **Platform:** A comfortable shoe with a thick, high heel.
- **Boots:** For a more daring look or great for a themed wedding.
- **Decorated white sneakers:** For maximum comfort.

Consider the length of your dress	If your gown is long and covers your shoes, you may be able to get away with one comfortable pair of shoes for the whole day. Whether you have one pair of shoes or two, make sure the dress is hemmed to the appropriate spot. Wear the shoes when your dress is being altered, so you'll know exactly where the hem falls.
Think about your skirt	An intricate shoe poking out from beneath a simple skirt is a beautiful touch. Or, if your skirt is intricate and decorated, go with a more understated shoe.
Prepare yourself	Even the most comfortable bridal shoes won't feel like running shoes, so get ready to sacrifice a modest amount of comfort for a fabulous shoe. To make your shoes extra comfy, buy them half a size bigger and stick a pad inside. A bridal salon consultant will help you choose a pad that's the right fit.
Prevent slippage	You may be taking the plunge, but you don't want to fall on your wedding day. You'll encounter some darn slippery surfaces, so ask the salesperson to abrade the soles to give them a little more traction.

GO GLAM WITH GLOVES

In the eighteenth and nineteenth centuries, gloves were given as a favor to all the wedding guests. Today, you can use them to add glamour and pizzazz to your wedding ensemble.

Long gloves are appropriate if your dress is short-sleeved or sleeveless, and they can reach to your mid-arm, elbow, or upper arm (called "opera" gloves), but you can also choose wrist-length gloves to go with a shorter sleeved dress if you so desire. If your dress is long-sleeved, go with gloves that end at your wrist.

Gloves are measured in terms of buttons. A wrist-length glove has one button; four-, six-, and eight-button gloves are all elbow length; and the most formal opera-style glove boasts sixteen buttons.

LEFT: *For a glamorous look, pair a long strapless dress with elbow-length gloves.*
FAR LEFT: *Black gloves paired with a crisp white gown can create contrast and drama.*

Fabric options for gloves include kid leather (the most formal); nylon; a cotton, nylon, and lace blend; stretch lace; crochet; and sheer nylon. Most gloves are white, but for a dramatic look, consider black gloves.

One thing to consider if you're wearing gloves is how you'll handle them during the ring ceremony. If you want to take your glove off, do it elegantly by gently tugging on each finger and then slowly sliding the glove off without turning it inside out. Or slit the underside of the ring finger of your glove, so you can poke your finger out when it's time for the ring. The ring can also be worn on a gloved fingertip until after the ceremony. It's up to you.

THE IMPERATIVE HANDBAG

Most women feel naked without a hand-bag—a feeling you don't want to encounter on your wedding day. So pick a pretty purse and pack it with all your essentials, from lipstick to tissues to your favorite fragrance.

Choose a handbag that matches your gown as closely as possible, or at least comple-ments its colors. There are a few basic styles of handbags that go well with almost any gown (again, as long as they match), including hard-sided, small satin clutch purses; beaded, egg-shaped purses; and satin drawstring pouches.

RIGHT: *A pretty purse packed with wedding day essentials, such as this hard-sided silver purse decorated with rhinestone, is a must for the bride.*

unveiled
FLOWER POWER

Flowers are a big part of wedding ceremonies and receptions. The groom is supposed to wear a flower that appears in the bridal bouquet in his buttonhole. This stems from the medieval tradition of a knight wearing his lady's colors to declare his love. Every flower has a special meaning and can display a particular message. An orange blossom, for example, signifies chastity, purity, and loveliness, while a red chrysanthemum means "I love you."

The Greeks, Persians, Indians, and Chinese all ascribed symbolic meanings to flowers. The wife of the British ambassador to the Turkish sultan's court, Lady Mary Wortley Montague, is credited with bringing the language of flowers to England in 1716. But it was the Victorians who grabbed the idea and turned it into a science, codifying every type of flower, leaf, grass, and herb, as well as their colors, combinations, and orientation.

The meaning of a flower changed depending on where it was worn. Even the type of ribbon and the way it was tied could turn a query into a refusal. A strategically arranged nosegay expressed emotion as explicitly—if not more so for the poetically challenged—as a handwritten note. And it could be surreptitious, too, because only those who knew the code could decipher the message. If a young lady received a bouquet of jonquils and snowdrops, she knew her suitor shared her affection and had hopes for a continued friendship. But should a woman return an ardent Romeo's orange roses (passion) to him with the blossoms facing down, no words were necessary to tell him to buzz off.

Use the flower meanings from the following list to create a bouquet, or apply them to a decorating scheme, using their colors and images throughout your reception hall. For example, energize the entry to the reception with hollyhock (ambition), lemon blossom (zest), clematis (ingenuity), and hepatica (confidence) —it couldn't hurt!

Acacia	**Friendship**
Azalea	**Temperance**
Bluebell	**Constancy**
Buttercup	**Youthfulness**
Camellia, red	**Excellence**
Chrysanthemum, white	**Optimism**
Cowslip	**Pensiveness**
Daffodil	**Regard**
Heliotrope	**Devotion**
Jasmine	**Cheerfulness**
Lilac	**Innocence**
Lotus	**Eloquence**
Oleander	**Caution**
Pansy	**Thoughtfulness**
Peony	**Bashfulness**
Thistle	**Austerity**
Violet, blue	**Modesty**

BUILDING THE FOUNDATION UNDER YOUR GOWN: UNDERGARMENTS

Years ago, a bride wore something under her wedding gown that she would later reveal to her new husband on their wedding night. This item was often bestowed upon the bride by her mother or grandmother.

A sweet, sentimental idea, but undergarments that offer necessary support and comfort aren't always the sexiest-looking ensembles. And let's face it: most lingerie items are too bulky and embellished to be worn under a sleek gown.

Today, most brides are putting practicality before fashion when choosing their undergarments; they want something that will hold them in tightly, no matter what it looks like when the dress comes off.

When you choose your undergarments, get the right pieces for your dress. Make sure no lines or bulges are visible underneath the dress and no fabric is peeking out above the back or neckline. Bridal salon consultants can help you with this.

And no matter how hot it is, always wear hose (unless, as we mentioned, you are wearing sandals or open-toed shoes). If it's a scorching July day, go with stockings and garters, which are cooler than pantyhose. And have at least three to five pairs of extra hose waiting on the sidelines in case of a snag.

Then, when the guests have all gone home and it's just you and your new husband, slip out of the girdle and rib-hugging bustier and into something sexy and sensual that's bound to send your new husband into a tizzy.

ONE WOMAN'S STORY

When I began the planning for my wedding, one of the most important elements to me was my wedding gown. I was willing to cut and save in virtually every aspect of the big day, OTHER than my gown. I had it all picked out in my head even before I went shopping. Something straight and beaded, lightweight for dancing throughout the night, and very flattering. My mother and I went to a variety of designer boutiques until we happened upon a shop with a gorgeous Badgley-Mischka gown—it was a silk sheath with a chantilly lace overlay, both of which were beaded with Austrian crystals and fresh-water pearls. I knew immediately it was to be my wedding gown. Much to my dismay, at my first fitting, the seamstress, being very blunt, slapped my butt and asked if I intended to lose 15 pounds before the big day. At that point, I hadn't really given it much thought and honestly, had planned on wearing some primitive torture device designed to minimize my, uh, flaws. I actually considered losing the weight, but things did not exactly go as planned. I brought my modern-day corset with me to my final fitting (I ended up having roughly six fittings in order to accommodate my rather generous proportions in the bust and rear nether-regions), and tried on my dress. I loved it! On the day of my wedding, I never felt so beautiful in my life. My only regret was the torturous corset I had chosen to wear, which became unbearably painful within several hours. I ended up removing it during the reception in the women's bathroom of the hotel, and walked out to enjoy the rest of my wedding night, pain-free, and looking as gorgeous as I did with the corset on!

–Andrea White, California

BELOW LEFT: *There's a perfect strapless bra for every strapless gown.*
BELOW RIGHT: *Even natural, princess silhouettes can use glamorous undergarments.*

Here comes the bride,
All dressed in white,
Sweetly, serenely in the soft glowing light.
Lovely to see, marching to thee,
Sweet love united for eternity.

—*"The Bridal Chorus," from the opera* Lohengrin,
Richard Wagner (1848)

Your special day is almost here, and of course you're ecstatic. You can't wait to begin the rest of your life.

As you well know, before you can start this new chapter of marital bliss, you must put on the performance of your life for your family and friends. Being the bride means more than just wearing the dress—you've got to become the bride and elegantly present yourself.

For an especially happy, healthy glow for your wedding, take care of yourself in the days leading up to it. Let's face it—these can be particularly stressful days. But you're well prepared, so things will go smoothly.

THE HOME STRETCH
During your last few days as a single woman, pamper yourself. Deep condition your hair for a few days in a row, give yourself a facial, and get a manicure. To prevent a disaster the morning of the wedding, practice doing your makeup or go through a trial run with your makeup artist. The more prepared you are, the more relaxed you'll be on the day of your wedding. Here are some other tips for the days leading up to the wedding:

TOP: *A bride prepares for one of the most important performances of her life in the moments before she walks down the aisle.*
BOTTOM: *If she makes the right choice, a bride's love of her gown will be as evident as her love for her husband.*
OPPOSITE: *Dressing for the wedding can be as special a ritual as the ceremony itself, both for a bride and her attendants.*

Don't overdo the tanning	Too-dark skin will distract from you and your dress. It's easy to get caught up in the "just back from the Bahamas" frenzy and end up looking more like a piece of mahogany furniture than a blushing bride. If you're really pale and self-conscious about your light skin tone, a little tanning shouldn't hurt, but err on the side of prudence.
Practice good posture	To get yourself ready for the hours of perfect posture you'll have to endure on the big day, practice with this pose: Sitting cross-legged on the floor, relax your shoulders (pull them down), raise your neck upward as if it's being lifted to the sky, pivot your hip bones forward, hold in your stomach muscles, and breathe. Another good exercise for posture: Stand on one foot and keep your back straight for 20 seconds—this forces balance. Also practice walking slowly and gracefully.
Cover tattoos	If you have a tattoo that's visible when you put on your dress, think about covering it for your wedding day, especially if it's on your back. If you don't cover it, you run the risk that your guests will pay more attention to the rose you chose ten years ago than the beautiful bride you are on your wedding day. Try a few different kinds of makeup to see which one gives the best coverage.
Give your dress a once-over	A few days before the wedding, pick up your dress from its final alteration. Once you get the dress home, take it out of the bag according to the instructions and inspect it for any flaws. If you find any imperfections or marks that you know weren't there when you bought it, take it back to the bridal salon or store to be cleaned or fixed.

ON THE BIG DAY

If the butterflies go haywire in your stomach at the mere thought of your wedding day, relax. These butterflies have a miraculous way of disappearing the moment you start walking down the aisle toward the man you love.

The single most important thing you can do on your wedding day is stay relaxed and stress-free. After all, this is the happiest day of your life. Don't let worries about perfect flower arrangements or over-imbibing friends ruin your high spirits.

The morning of the wedding, eat something healthful yet substantial that will sustain you for hours without giving you indigestion on top of an already nervous stomach.

Then inspect your gown one more time. If you see wrinkles, press it according to the instructions. For instance, silk dresses should only be pressed with a dry iron, because water will leave marks. If your veil is wrinkled, hang it in the bathroom when you take a shower—the steam will smooth it out.

When it's time to get dressed, put your shoes and garter on before you slip into the gown. Have your makeup done before you dress, but be extra careful to keep your face away from your gown as you put it on to avoid any smears or stains. Attach your headpiece and/or veil last, after your hair is done, and stick combs in your hair against the direction of hair growth for a more secure fit.

In case something does go awry, pack a wedding day survival kit that includes mouthwash for fresh breath, extra panty hose and clear nail polish in case of a snag, nail glue for manicure problems, pain-killers, deodorant, and Band-Aids.

On the way to the ceremony—where you will unveil yourself and your dress—move carefully and slowly, and if at all possible, try not to sit on the back of your gown.

RIGHT: *A bride takes a few practice steps in her gown.*

During the ceremony, relax and be graceful. Saunter or stroll down the aisle, with your bouquet held at the level of your belly button, so your guests will see the beautiful bodice and neckline of your dress. Brides who hold their bouquets white-knuckled at their chests not only appear tense but they also hide their gowns. And remember to breathe!

Also, stand up straight. Your mother was right—good posture will make you look taller, leaner, more radiant, and more confident. To achieve good posture, keep your back straight when you walk and sit. Stand comfortably and pull your shoulders back (keeping them relaxed), pull in your stomach and keep your abdominal muscles taut, lift your chest out of your ribs, and raise your head so that the bottom of your chin is parallel to the ground.

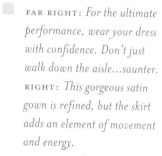

FAR RIGHT: *For the ultimate performance, wear your dress with confidence. Don't just walk down the aisle...saunter.*
RIGHT: *This gorgeous satin gown is refined, but the skirt adds an element of movement and energy.*
OPPOSITE: *Good posture makes a bride appear taller, leaner, and more confident.*

In addition, watch the fidgeting (mom was right yet again!). If you're wearing a strapless dress, don't continuously yank the top up to make sure you're covered—this is almost as bad as pulling material out of your rear end. Build the right foundation with undergarments that will hold your dress in place in all the right places.

Throughout the entire day and night, you're bound to be smiling from ear to ear. To avoid a painful jaw the next day, take breaks from smiling when no one is looking and periodically massage your facial muscles.

To prevent a disastrous dress stain, stick with clear beverages, such as white wine and water, and steer clear of red wine, coffee, and dark soda. Although you may be able to chug beers with the best of them on a typical Saturday night, forego the beer bottle and drink from a glass for the night.

Most important, have the time of your life on your wedding day. If you're beaming, your husband and your guests will notice and feel your positive energy, and they'll have an enchanted time as well. A blissful bride makes for a perfect wedding.

WHY CAN'T THE GROOM SEE YOU BEFORE THE WEDDING?

Traditionally, brides have been thought to be particularly vulnerable to evil spirits, and many of the customs and traditions associated with weddings are meant to provide protection. The veil was originally worn by Roman brides. It was thought that it would disguise the bride and therefore outwit malevolent spirits. The veil became popular in Britain during the nineteenth century. In the United States, it is associated with modesty and chastity. In some Eastern ceremonies, the bride is veiled and the groom is not allowed to see the bride's face until after the wedding ceremony. In some Jewish weddings there is a ritual where the groom ensures that the bride is his intended before placing the veil over her face.

Most couples are aware of the unspoken rule that the groom should not see the bride in her gown before the wedding day, but did you know that in Ireland the bride shouldn't see her entire reflection in a mirror while wearing her bridal gown either? If she does see herself in her entirety, it is believed that part of her will stay in her old life and not move on with her new life. If either of these rules is broken, the wedding is usually put off for an entire year.

ONE WOMAN'S STORY

Nicole fell in love with the first dress she tried on. It was everything she ever imagined her wedding dress would be—understated yet elegant. Of course, Nicole abided by the rules and tried a number of other dresses on as well, but she kept going back to that first one.

And it was a gorgeous dress indeed—a princess cut with a tasteful, sleeveless, embroidered bodice and delicate illusion netting that rose to the neckline.

Nicole's dress worked out wonderfully on her wedding day. She felt like a princess, and she was totally comfortable. Then, just as she was about to leave the dressing room, one bridesmaid asked another bridesmaid for a bottle of nail polish that was sitting on a counter.

The bridesmaid passed the bottle across Nicole's dress and… the bottle spilled…red nail polish all over the front of the dress… about a half-hour before the ceremony was set to begin.

Someone called the bridal shop and a saleswoman rushed over with cleaning fluid and an extra dress (just in case). The cleaning fluid didn't get the entire stain out, and the saleswoman had to pin a little piece of fabric over the stain, but by the time the bride walked down the aisle she was completely composed and looked beautiful, as a friend of the bride attested. She was such a happy bride that if you didn't know what had happened, the friend said, you would have never guessed either from looking at her dress or from seeing her smiling face.

Now that's what I call bridal style.

–Elizabeth Shimer, Pennsylvania

WEDDING GOWN CHECKLIST

*Bring this checklist with you on all of your outings—
you'll never forget to ask the right questions!*

the wedding gown book

"The rule should be that after you're married, you get to wear your wedding dress to every wedding you attend. The only woman who wouldn't understand would be the bride, and she would understand the next day."

—Renée James, a bride on October 18, 1986

ABOUT THE GOWN

Is it appropriate?

Is it in my price range?

Is it comfortable to sit in?

Is it comfortable to hug in?

Is it comfortable to dance in?

Is this a style I would
normally wear?

Is it figure flattering?

What does everyone else think?

Month-by-Month Shopping Planner

9 to 12 MONTHS BEFORE THE BIG DAY

- **Start doing your homework.** Research bridal salons, flip through bridal magazines, begin creating a scrapbook of looks you like or would like to imitate.

- **Start shopping or meet with a seamstress.**

6 to 9 MONTHS BEFORE THE BIG DAY

- **Have "the one" picked out.**

4 to 6 MONTHS BEFORE THE BIG DAY

- **Choose and order your veil and/or headpiece.**

- **Shop for your undergarments, shoes, and accessories.**

2 MONTHS BEFORE THE BIG DAY

- **Schedule your fitting appointments.**

- **Start brainstorming hairstyles and makeup.**

1 MONTH BEFORE THE BIG DAY

- **Schedule your final fitting.** Take your maid of honor with you so she can learn her duties: to straighten your train, bustle your gown, fluff your veil, and secure your headpiece. Your final fitting should be a week or two before the wedding—a lot can happen in a month!

ABOVE: *On the big day, you can congratulate yourself for having survived months of planning and preparation.*
OPPOSITE: *A bride knows she's chosen the right dress when she feels absolutely fabulous in it.*

RESOURCES

united states

Joyce Scardina Becker, CMP
Events of Distinction
t: 415.751.0211 / 866.99.EVENT (toll-free)
e: joyce@eventsofdistinction.com
www.eventsofdistinction.com

Based in San Francisco, CA, Joyce Scardina Becker is the president of Events of Distinction, an innovative wedding design company that won the 2003 WESTIE Award for Best Wedding Over $100,000; the director of the Wedding Consultant Certificate Program at California State University, Hayward, the first wedding certificate program offered on a university campus; and the wedding expert for www.theknot.com, www.abc7news.com, and www.leadingcaterers.com.

Yolanda Cellucci
Yolanda's
355 Waverly Oaks Road
Waltham, MA 02452
t: 781.899.6480

Yolanda's is a boutique bridal shop well known throughout New England.

Allison Dickson
e: aldickson@att.net,
jurezzio@theideanetwork.net
www.thea-list.com

Stylist Allison Dickson has more than 13 years of experience and expertise in fashion, accessories, style, design, and still and television production. The A-List is a website devoted to sharing information and spotting trends throughout these industries.

Elaine's of Edmonds
610 Main Street
Edmonds, WA 98020
t: 425.778.1814 / f: 425.774.3899
www.elaines.com

Elaine's of Edmonds is Seattle's premier bridal shop and has been in business since 1979 serving the Pacific Northwest and beyond.

Sharon Naylor
e: slnaylor@optonline.net

Sharon Naylor is the author of 18 wedding planning books, the wedding Q&A specialist at NJWedding.com, and is a regular contributor to the top bridal magazines, including *Bridal Guide*, *Bride Again*, and *Bride's*. She has also written for *Shape*, *Health*, *Self*, *Woman's Day*, *Cosmopolitan*, and dozens of other national magazines, and her wedding and fashion articles have been syndicated by Copley News Service.

Priscilla of Boston
40 Cambridge Street
Charlestown, MA 02129
t: 617.242.2677 / f: 617.242.9244
www.priscillaofboston.com

Priscilla of Boston has boutiques throughout the U.S., including Dallas and Denver.

Marianne Shearer
The Dresser
Fullerton, CA 92832
t: 714.870.7101
e: thedresser@earthlink.net

Marianne Shearer is the owner of a boutique bridal shop.

Crys Stewart
Wedding Bells
e: info@weddinggazette.com

Crys Stewart is the editor-in-chief of the magazine *Wedding Bells*.

Danielle Turcola
Professionalism International
Twinsburg, OH 44087
t: 330.963.0011
e: Danielle@AskDanielle.com
www.danielleturcola.com

Danielle Turcola is a professional presence consultant.

Anna Soo Wildermuth, IACI, CIP
Personal Images Inc.
t: 630.530.0951
e: anna@personalimagesinc.com
www.personalimagesinc.com

Anna Soo Wildermuth is a certified image professional.

BOOKS

If you are interested in incorporating traditional—or nontraditional—elements into your ceremony, these books will offer plenty of food for thought. Any bookstore will have shelves devoted to wedding guides and literature. Dig in!

Alternative Weddings: An Essential Guide for Creating Your Own Ceremonies, Jane Ross-MacDonald

The Essential Guide to Lesbian and Gay Weddings, Tess Ayersa and Paul Brown

Joining Hands and Hearts: Interfaith, Intercultural Wedding Celebrations—A Practical Guide for Couples, Susanna Stefanachi Macomb

Jumping the Broom: The African-American Wedding Planner, Harriette Cole

The Knot Guide to Wedding Vows and Traditions: Readings, Rituals, Music, Dances, and Toasts, Carley Roney with *The Knot*

The New Jewish Wedding, Revised, Anita Diamant

Viva el Amor/Long Live Love: The Latino Wedding Planner: A Guide to Planning a Traditional Ceremony and a Fabulous Fiesta, Edna R. Bautista

Weddings from the Heart: Contemporary and Traditional Ceremonies for an Unforgettable Wedding, Daphne Rose Kingma

Wedding Readings: Centuries of Writing and Rituals on Love and Marriage, edited by Eleanor C. Munro

ONLINE RESOURCES

From gowns and flowers to rings and global traditions, you can find nearly anything you're looking for on the Web. This is just the tip of the iceberg that is online wedding resources.

House of Brides

www.houseofbrides.com

House of Brides is an online retailer with a wide selection of wedding gowns and designer wedding dresses, as well as dresses and accessories for all the attendants.

Organic Weddings

www.organicweddings.com

Organic Weddings' mission statement is to promote "eco-friendly and socially responsible events that balance style, ecology, and tradition." They are a comprehensive wedding planning resource for couples striving to live healthy, natural lifestyles with respect for the environment.

Tekay Designs

www.tk-designs.com

Tekay Designs specializes in maternity clothing, plus sizes, African and ethnic wear, and carries one of the largest selections of wedding dresses, wedding gowns, maternity clothes, maternity wedding dresses, bridesmaids dresses, and evening and formal wear in the U.S. They have a new African and ethnic bridal collection tailored for customers who want an Afrocentric wedding or African-inspired wedding attire. They also custom make clothes for plus-, unusual-, and standard-size customers.

WeddingChannel.com

www.weddingchannel.com

This website has a gowns and dresses finder and showcases more than 100 designers' creations for brides, bridesmaids, flower girls, and mothers of the bride. There is also a resource listing for local services in your region.

united kingdom

PUBLICATIONS

Bride & Groom

Aim Publications Ltd
31-35 Beak Street
London, W1R 3LD
t: +44 020 7440 3848

I do!

First Press Publishing
40 Anderson Quay
Glasgow G2 4HU
t: +44 0141 242 1400
e: ido@dailyrecord.co.uk

London Wedding

Aim Publications Ltd
31-35 Beak Street
London, W1R 3LD
t: +44 020 7440 3800
e: info@londonwedding.co.uk

The Scottish Wedding Directory

Unit 21, Six Harmony Row
Glasgow G51 3BA
t: +44 0141 445 5545
e: scotwed.dir@virgin.net

Wedding & Home

IPC Magazines
Kings Reach Tower, Stamford Street
London SE1 9LS
t: +44 020 7261 747

You & Your Wedding

Aim Publications Ltd
31-35 Beak Street
London W1R 3LD
t: +44 020 7440 3838
e: info@youandyourwedding.co.uk

ONLINE RESOURCES

Confetti.co.uk

www.confetti.co.uk
Online community that offers regular newsletters; search engines for wedding venues and honeymoon destinations; free samples of catalogs and stationery; event suppliers directories throughout the UK; and buying guides for bridal wear and accessories.

WeddingGuideUK.com

www.weddingguideuk.com
Provides in-depth articles that offer advice, ideas, and inspiration on all aspects of the wedding; hosts discussion forums; features a special section for the groom and his attendants.

Wedding-Service-UK

www.wedding-service.co.uk
A jam-packed, no-frills guide to everything bridal in the UK; an excellent starting point for extensive local listings.

WedUK

Wedding Services Directory
www.weduk.com
An all-encompassing directory of retailers, venues, wedding advice, and more. Includes links to resources in the Republic of Ireland as well.

CONTRIBUTOR CREDITS

Many thanks to the people who lent family photographs for the writing of this book:

Elmer and Prudence Beal

Helen Beal

Gerald and Barbara Burton

Michael and Odette Gornick

Robert and Rachel Guerin

Christopher and Katherine Hart

Suzanne Madeira

Mary Ahern Mears

Susan Mears

David and Leah Rogers

Amy Kuschel Bride
23 Grant Avenue
San Francisco, CA 94108 USA
t: 415.956.5657 / f: 415.956.5627
e: info@amykuschel.com
www.amykuschel.com

72 (right), 77 (top right)

Anne Barge, Inc.
75 14th Street NE , Suite 2710
Atlanta, GA 30309 USA
t: 404.873.8070 / f: 404.873.8074
www.annebarge.com

31 (left), 38 (left), 41 (right), 45 (bottom left), 54 (middle), 56 (right), 77 (third and fourth from top, left), 96, 113 (top), 114 (top and bottom), 115 (both), 122 (bottom), 126 (right), 131 (bottom), 136

Bachrach Inc.
www.bachrachstudios.com

10, 11 (top)

Bananas
Richard Leonard
78 Main Street
Gloucester, MA 01930 USA
t: 978.283.8806
vintage and consignment clothing

20 (all)

Jennifer K. Beal
www.jkbealphoto.com

18, 142

Christos Inc.
241 West 37th Street
New York, NY 10018 USA
t: 212.921.0025 / f: 212.921.0127
www.christosbridal.com

118

Dessy
118 West 20th Street
New York, NY 10011 USA
www.dessy.com
www.aftersix.com

27 (left), 40 (top), 45 (middle right), 56 (left), 67, 74, 80 (both), 82 (right), 83 (right), 84, 85 (bottom right), 100, 101, 104

ABOUT THE AUTHOR

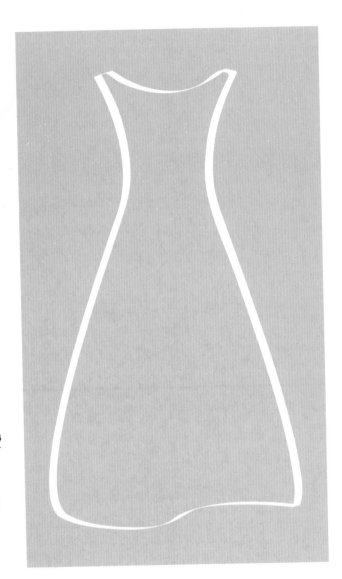

Elizabeth Shimer

is a freelance writer who specializes in women's
issues, from relationships to fashion. She lives
in Bethlehem, Pennsylvania.